Praise for Around the Catholic Table

"We love this cookbook! Emily has turned us into a risotto family. We often make her risotto when we host, and we always receive so many compliments. There's nothing like a simple one-pot dish to serve a crowd. Emily has taken the stress out of hosting with so many simple yet elevated recipes that are sure to be a hit every time. She has thought of every detail, and her heart behind hospitality is the icing on the cake. This cookbook has blessed our family and all those whom we welcome into our home to feed."

Stephanie, wife and mother to three young boys

"This is one of the main recipe collections we use on a regular basis. I probably cook at least one dish from it every week. My family loves everything we've tried, especially the soups and risottos. With lots of seasonal variety and allergy-free recipes, this cookbook is helpful when we need a good go-to recipe for friends or family members with dietary restrictions. Emily's delicious recipes and beautiful writing about the sacramentality of food have helped me grow from a reluctant cook to someone who finds joy in the creativity of the kitchen."

JoAnna, librarian and mother of three

"It's a rare cookbook that feeds both a clamoring family and a bustling table of guests with ease, but Emily manages this feat with her hearty and homey recipes. You know those cookbooks that contain more misses than hits? Not this one. Every recipe works, and they are universally loved—a miracle! She's the undisputed Queen of Risotto, and her precise directions have given me the confidence to host friends while casually stirring rice with one hand and sipping from a glass of wine in the other. Three cheers for Emily!"

Cyndi, cookbook author

"What a blessing this cookbook has been for us! I start with *Around the Catholic Table* to find achievable, allergen-free recipes for company and weeknight dinner ideas I know the whole family will love. Plus, the pumpkin bread and pumpkin cheesecake have already become traditions for our Thanksgiving. I thought the book would have ten or so great recipes we would dust off a couple times a year. Instead, it has become a go-to cookbook on my kitchen counter."

Brianna, child welfare attorney and mother of two

"Consistently, Emily's cookbook is the one I look to the most. Her balanced philosophy of hospitality and realistic expectations shines beautifully (and deliciously) through each recipe."

Theresa, English professor and mother of four

"The essay discussing Emily's approach to food allergies has been so helpful since I love making meals for people. It gave me the confidence to offer meals to friends with allergies when they have new babies, have lost a loved one, or are dealing with other life challenges. This cookbook is a gift to the world and would make a perfect bridal shower or wedding gift."

Catherine, lover of food and mother of two

"Through a series of well-written essays and crowd-tested recipes, Emily offers the Catholic homemaker a firm but gentle challenge to see their home and their cooking anew—as a place where true friendships can take root and flourish and the Gospel can be lived out together. Her essays address every major objection or hesitancy a person might have, and her delicious recipes are easy to follow. I would encourage every Catholic to have a copy on hand and step into the joy that comes when we invite our neighbors over for dinner."

Jessica, fertility awareness educator and mother of six

AROUND THE CATHOLIC TABLE

EMILY STIMPSON CHAPMAN

AROUND THE CATHOLIC TABLE

100+ Simple Recipes for Family and Friends

Steubenville, Ohio
www.emmausroad.org

Emmaus Road Publishing
1380 University Blvd.
Steubenville, Ohio 43952

Printed in the United States of America

First printing 2025

Library of Congress Control Number: 2025940098

ISBN: 978-1-64585-491-3 Hardcover | 978-1-64585-492-0 Paperback | 978-1-64585-493-7 Ebook

Cover design and layout by Emily Muse Morelli

Photography by Caitlin Renn

Additional photography by Emily Stimpson Chapman

For the Thursday Night Dinner Crew,
with all my love.

CONTENTS

SIDES 213

DESSERTS 237

COCKTAILS

INTRODUCTION

The Gift of Hospitality

My parents gave my sisters and me many gifts, but one of the greatest was a love of easy, casual, no muss, no fuss hospitality.

When I was growing up, hardly a week went by when my parents' siblings or friends didn't come over to our house for dinner or when we didn't go over to their houses for the same. Weekends inevitably meant hanging out with the aunts and uncles or my parents' best friends, the Moores, the Arnolds, and the Cabays. The adults would gather in one room, the kids would gather in another, and parties lasted late into the night—with every corner of the hosting home filled with conversation, laughter, and shouts of children at play.

That was in the winter months, though. During the spring, summer, and fall, we would take our "Whole Gang Parties" outside, where the kids ran through ravines and played games of freeze tag on hilltops while the adults talked and drank beer on the deck.

> ***We weren't there to inspect how well the beds were made. We were there to be with each other, to love each other and be loved by each other, to talk about what had happened during the week, and to forget for just a few hours about the stresses that awaited us in the weeks ahead.***

There was always food at those parties: sometimes take-out pizza, other nights burgers or lasagna or a big pot of chili. But nothing was complicated. Nothing was fancy. Nothing would have merited its own photo shoot for Pinterest.

The houses were also a far cry from what you see on Instagram today. The furniture was beaten and battered from children's games. Bedrooms were usually a mess. And I'm sure, if I had cared enough to look, dust bunnies lurked in every corner.

But I didn't care. Nor did anyone else. We weren't there to inspect how well the beds were made. We were there to be with each other, to love each other and be loved by each other, to talk about what had happened during the week, and to forget for just a few hours about the stresses that awaited us in the weeks ahead.

The memories of those happy nights are among the best from my childhood. Those memories also continue to inspire me every time I invite friends or strangers over for dinner. From my parents, I learned the power of hospitality. I saw how it could build community, stave off loneliness, and fill homes with joy—making our days richer and our nights shorter. I also learned that hospitality doesn't have to be complicated or require Herculean efforts of cooking and cleaning.

The Spirit of Hospitality

For nearly thirty years now, I have been putting into practice all the lessons in hospitality that my parents, their siblings, and their friends taught me. Almost every week (often more than once a week), I open the door to my home so that others can eat around my table. Sometimes I'm just cooking for one guest. Other times, I'm cooking for two hundred. But the same spirit that animated those weekend get-togethers of my childhood animates the hosting and cooking I do in my own home now.

The food might be simple, but it will always be ample. I can never promise that the bedrooms will be clean, but I can promise that your glass won't go empty. I can also promise that the conversation will be real. If I've had a good day or a good week, I'll tell you all about it. If I've had a bad day or a bad week, I'll tell you all about that, too. I am always me when I'm hosting. There is no acting, no pretention, no trying to impress.

What I've come to see, through two decades of cooking and hosting, is that hospitality is one of the ways we can answer the Church's call to be open to life.

When you come into my house, you're coming into my world, with all its joys and sorrows. And my prayer is that by being real with you, I'm giving you the space to be real too—to tell me about your good days and bad days, to share your joys and sorrows, to be yourself, to be at home in my home.

That's what everyone needs: not five-star dining but a place where they're always welcome and where they can experience a foretaste of the heavenly banquet to which each of us is called.

What I've come to see, through two decades of cooking and hosting, is that hospitality is one of the ways we can answer the Church's call to be open to life. Not everyone can have babies. Not everyone can adopt them either. But everyone with a home can invite a friend to dinner. Everyone with a stove can open their doors to someone in need of a meal and some good conversation. Everyone with a kitchen table can give someone a seat of their own, even if just for a few hours.

When we do that, we welcome life into our homes. We're saying yes to the needs, problems, and messes of the other. And, in return, we're receiving the gifts, beauty, and joy of the other.

Is this act of welcoming always convenient? No. Is it often humbling? Totally. Is it sometimes stressful? Definitely. Even messy, casual, far-from-Pinterest-Perfect entertaining comes with hassles. But is the life hospitality inevitably brings into our homes worth the occasional stress and inconvenience? Always.

And that brings us to the purpose of this book.

About This Book

When Chris and I married and bought our first home together, we knew we wanted to fill it with life. We wanted friends, family, and children of friends and family sitting around our table. We also wanted our children sitting around the table. We expected those children would be born of our bodies, but those bodies did not cooperate. It was a great grief at the time—the greatest grief I had ever experienced to that point. But, with grace, infertility became an occasion for the greatest of blessings. It led us, one by one, to our three children—Toby, Becket, and Ellie—who came to us because of the loving choices of their first mothers: first to give them life and then to entrust them to us through adoption.

This cookbook, which you are holding in your hands, helped bring our two youngest home. We spent every penny we had adopting our first son, Toby. We had no money for a second adoption. But we didn't feel like our family was complete. Someone was missing. So I came up with an idea. I would write an e-cookbook filled with my simplest, tastiest, and most crowd-friendly recipes for hosting. Then anyone who wanted to contribute to our adoption fundraiser would get a cookbook as a thank you. Chris and I hoped and prayed it would work. And it did. Amazingly so. Not only did it help us fund Becket's adoption, but when we discovered one month after his birth that our oldest son's birth parents were expecting again and wanted us to adopt the new baby, it helped us fund her adoption as well.

My family was doubly blessed by this cookbook, and for that, I suppose it will always be my most favorite of all my books. Many other families were blessed by it too—so much so that not a week went by without someone asking if I had any plans to publish it as a physical book. The answer was always no. I was just too busy with so many little ones so close in age.

In the summer of 2024, however, the time finally seemed right to revisit the idea. I liked the idea of turning my little e-cookbook into a real book, but I wanted to do more than just that. I also wanted to expand it with new recipes, new essays, and new photos. Which is exactly what I've done.

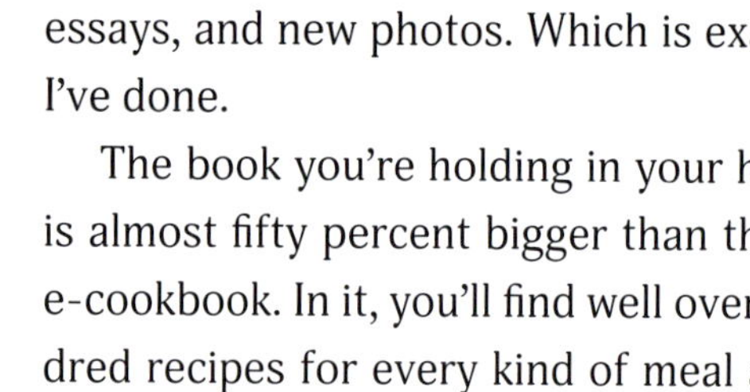

The book you're holding in your hands now is almost fifty percent bigger than the original e-cookbook. In it, you'll find well over one hundred recipes for every kind of meal and party, from Sunday brunches to Saturday night suppers to fast weeknight dinners and cocktails to share in the kitchen with friends. Almost all the recipes are my own, with a few coming from family and friends and a few more inspired by other people's recipes. Almost all are likewise designed to feed a crowd of at least eight, but most can be easily doubled, tripled, or quadrupled. I know this because I've quadrupled nearly all of them over the years. All are also designed to make hosting easy: most either can be made ahead and kept warm until company arrives or popped into the oven well in advance of the doorbell ringing. I've included tips throughout the book to help you plan and time your cooking accordingly.

Similarly, the recipes are designed to make hosting safe for guests with allergies. In recent years, one of the biggest impediments to hospitality in the United States has been the proliferation of food allergies and special diets. For a family that lives on pasta, cooking for guests who eat gluten-free can feel more than a little intimidating. So to make this easier, I've included recipes in every section that take into account the most common food allergies and dietary restrictions. Many recipes are gluten-free. There also are dairy free recipes, vegetarian and vegan recipes, and nut-free recipes. All these designations are clearly noted at the top of each recipe.

The only section that doesn't feature a dairy-free, vegan friendly recipe is the section on risottos. There may be a way to make risotto without butter and cheese, but it's not one I feel good recommending! I did, however, include a one-thousand-word essay on cooking risotto. I know: I have issues. But risotto is my favorite meal to cook for family and friends, and while it's not typically an *easy* recipe for entertaining, it can be once you figure out how to approach it in the context of hospitality. Hence, my one-thousand-word essay.

In addition to the risotto manifesto, I've included nine additional essays: one on the Catholic understanding of food, another on food and the feminine genius, and seven on the more practical aspects of hosting—cooking for guests with food allergies, preparing for guests observing a special diet, getting the house ready, feeding dinner to other people's children, feeding your own children, hosting when space and budgets are limited, and hosting when you have a little one (or many little ones) of your own. I hope these essays both open your heart to welcoming more people into your home and make it easier for you to do so.

A Distinction that Matters

Before moving on to the recipes, though, I want to make one important distinction about the focus of this book. It's not a handbook for "entertaining." It's a handbook for *hospitality*. There is a difference. Entertaining is about impressing people; hospitality is about loving people. Entertaining is about you; hospitality is about others. Entertaining requires time and money; hospitality requires vulnerability and an open door. Entertaining is for those who enjoy it; hospitality is for everyone.

> ***Entertaining is about impressing people; hospitality is about loving people. Entertaining is about you; hospitality is about others.***

Each of us has something to offer one another, and what we have to offer doesn't depend on how big our house is, how clean our floors are, or how fancy our cooking is. It depends on our willingness to let people into our homes, be real with them, and love them where they are. It depends on us setting aside our own insecurities and fears so we can make room for another.

My parents' willingness to do that was a gift to them and to my sisters and me. It showed us how rich and beautiful a life lived in community could be. It witnessed to us what real friendship and hospitality look like. It also laid a foundation for healthy marriages and for a life of faith, centered on a relationship with Jesus Christ, experienced in the community of the Church.

I pray that this book helps you give your family and friends that same gift. I also pray that it helps you find the same joy in welcoming others that hospitality has helped me find.

Notes on Cooking for People with Food Allergies

As someone with an anaphylactic peanut allergy, I get how serious food allergies can be. So before anyone comes to my house for dinner, I take the following precautions:

1. ***Ask:*** Whenever new guests are coming to dinner, I check with them about any food restrictions they might have. I also ask about the severity of the restriction. Is it an allergy, a sensitivity, or a preference? If it's an allergy, is it airborne? Do I need to worry about cross-contamination of cooking equipment or equipment on which food might have been manufactured?

2. ***Clean:*** If cross-contamination is an issue, I make sure to sanitize, in the dishwasher, any pots, pans, dishes, or utensils that I plan on using. I also clean my cutting surfaces with a disinfectant that includes bleach and do the same for any areas where little ones might have smeared nut butters.

3. ***Read labels:*** Peanuts, soy, corn, and gluten lurk in the strangest of places, so read all the labels of any products you might be using to make sure everything is free of particular food allergens.

4. ***Menu plan carefully:*** If the allergy is airborne, it's important that the entire menu be completely free of that ingredient. My sister, who has celiac disease, is fine if other people are eating bread or pasta when she is in the room. With my peanut allergy, though, it's important that there not be a peanut in sight. Plan your menu accordingly.

5. ***When in doubt, ask again:*** People with serious food allergies don't mind answering your questions about what they can and can't eat. They appreciate you taking their lives seriously! So if you're confused or uncertain or just want to double-check that something is safe, don't hesitate to give them a call or send them a text to clarify. More often than not, that call will save you worry and time!

Note: Unless otherwise stated, all recipes call for kosher salt. I typically use Morton's Kosher Salt. If you use Diamond Kosher Salt, you will need to use a bit more than when using Morton's. All baking recipes use iodized salt.

ALLERGEN KEY

GF = Gluten-Free

DF = Dairy-Free

V = Vegetarian

VG = Vegan

NF = Nut Free

An * indicates that a recipe can be made allergen-friendly with modifications.

Thirty-Minute Meals

Here are my go-to recipes for busy days when there's no time to cook but the people in my house still insist on eating. All these recipes take about thirty minutes from start to finish (depending on how many babies want to be held or sibling fights I need to referee), and are eaten happily, on average, by at least four out of five Chapmans.

BRUNCH

Sunday brunch is always one of the easiest meals to host because you can make so much of the food in advance. A typical brunch menu at my house involves one or two of the dishes included in this chapter, which I prepare the night before, bake before leaving for church, and then keep warm in the oven.

Also on the table you'll find fruit salad, muffins or a pastry (store-bought unless someone else volunteers to bring some), maybe bagels with lox and cream cheese, plus beverages: most likely coffee, juice, and the fixings for Mimosas and Bloody Marys.

Nothing is complicated or overly elegant, but friends still gather and children still play. Which is, of course, the point of it all.

APPLE GRANOLA CRISP

GF, V	Serves: 8	Prep Time: 30 minutes	Cook Time: 45–50 minutes

I am a firm believer that if you top a fruit crisp with yogurt instead of ice cream, it is a breakfast food, not a dessert. Not everyone is as convinced of this as I am, though, so for this breakfast treat I lightened up the amount of sugar I normally put in fruit crisps and added good-for-you ingredients like coconut, almonds, and almond meal to the oat topping. We serve this for brunches, but it also makes a fantastic weekday breakfast.

- 3 pounds (roughly 9 cups) apples, peeled, cored, and cut into medium chunks
- 2 tablespoons orange juice
- 4 tablespoons sugar
- 2 tablespoons cornstarch
- 1 teaspoon cinnamon
- 1 cup butter
- 1/4 cup brown sugar
- 1/2 cup almond meal
- 2 cups old-fashioned oats (gluten-free if needed)
- 1/2 cup sliced almonds
- 1/2 cup unsweetened shredded coconut
- 1/4 teaspoon salt, divided
- 4 cups or 1 (32 ounce) container of yogurt (Greek, plain whole milk, vanilla, or honey)

1. Preheat oven to 350° F.
2. In a 9 x 13-inch baking dish, mix apples with orange juice, sugar, cornstarch, cinnamon, and a pinch of salt. Toss until coated.
3. In a medium saucepan, melt butter with brown sugar. Add almond meal, oats, almonds, coconut, and a pinch of salt. Stir until clumpy.
4. Spread topping over the apple mixture and bake for 45–50 minutes, until the apples are softened and bubbly and crust is golden brown.
5. Serve either hot or cold, with yogurt.

BACON, HAM & CHEDDAR CRUSTLESS QUICHE

GF, NF	Serves: 8	Prep Time: 10 minutes	Cook Time: 45 minutes

Three weeks after Toby was born, my husband's relatives from Florida came into town. I hosted brunch. Everyone thought I was insane. Maybe I was. But either way, it unfolded smoothly, thanks to this easy-peasy crustless quiche, which you can either prep in ten minutes and bake or prepare the night before and then pop into the oven the next morning.

6 eggs
1 cup milk
1 cup grated cheddar cheese
1 cup cubed ham
4 slices bacon, cooked crisp and crumbled
3 tablespoons chives
1 teaspoon salt
freshly ground black pepper to taste

1. Preheat oven to 350° F.
2. Whisk together the milk, eggs, cheese, salt, and pepper. Add ham to egg mixture and gently stir.
3. Pour egg mixture into a lightly greased 9-inch pie pan and sprinkle chives and bacon on top of egg mixture.
4. At this point, you can bake the quiche immediately or cover with plastic wrap and refrigerate overnight.
5. Bake uncovered for about 35–45 minutes or until the center is set.
6. Serve hot or at room temperature.

ELIZABETH SCALIA'S BAKED OATMEAL

GF, V, NF*	Serves: 8–10	Prep Time: 10 minutes	Bake Time: 40–50 minutes

Decades ago, Catholic writer Elizabeth Scalia shared a recipe for baked oatmeal on her blog. I adapted it to my liking and have been using it to feed houseguests (and now my family) for close to twenty years. It's best when assembled the night before then baked before houseguests get out of bed, but it also can be thrown together quickly in the morning and baked immediately. Either way, the smell is a fantastic alarm clock.

3 cups old-fashioned oats (gluten-free if needed)

1 cup brown sugar

3 teaspoons cinnamon

2 teaspoons baking powder

1 teaspoon salt

1 cup milk

2 eggs

1/2 cup plus 3 tablespoons melted butter

2 teaspoons vanilla extract

1 cup raisins

1 cup chopped walnuts (optional)

4 apples, cored and sliced

2 teaspoons pumpkin pie spice

about 1 cup heavy cream

1. In a large bowl, mix together oats, brown sugar, 2 teaspoons of the cinnamon, baking powder, and salt.
2. In a separate bowl, beat milk, eggs, melted butter, and vanilla extract.
3. Pour the wet ingredients into the dry ingredients and combine. Then stir in raisins and walnuts.
4. Spread into a buttered 9 x 13-inch baking dish, cover with plastic wrap, and refrigerate overnight.
5. In the morning, preheat oven to 350° F and bake the oatmeal for 35–45 minutes or until fork comes out clean.
6. While oatmeal bakes, cut and core the apples. In a large frying pan, melt 3 tablespoons of butter. Add apples, pumpkin pie spice, and remaining teaspoon of cinnamon. Cook until soft (8–12 minutes). Keep warm until ready to serve.
7. When oatmeal is done, cover with foil to keep warm or serve immediately, topped with spiced apples and a drizzle of cream (1–2 tablespoons per serving).

CHRISTINA'S SCONES

V, NF	Makes 12 scones	Prep Time: 10 minutes	Bake Time: 12–15 minutes

I love my friend Christina. She is kind, thoughtful, intelligent, and adored by small children everywhere. Even if she didn't make the world's most amazing scones, I would invite her to every brunch I host. But the opposite is also true. Even if she weren't one of the loveliest people I know, I would still invite her to brunch for these scones alone.

3 cups flour
1/2 cup sugar
1 teaspoon salt
2 1/2 teaspoons baking powder
1/2 teaspoon baking soda
3/4 cup butter, frozen
1 cup plus 4 tablespoons buttermilk

Additions (choose one or a combination):

3 tablespoons orange zest
3 tablespoons lemon zest
1 cup chocolate chips
1/2 cup fresh fruit, diced

1. Preheat oven to 400° F and line two baking two sheets with parchment paper.
2. Combine dry ingredients. Grate or cut butter into small cubes and slowly add to the dry ingredients. Using your hands, work the butter until the texture becomes coarse, with the flour forming chickpea-sized balls.
3. Make a well in the middle of the flour mixture and pour buttermilk into the well. Stir until a dough forms, but don't overmix.
4. Add additions as desired, stirring until just mixed.
5. Divide dough in two on a floured surface. Briefly knead each half.
6. Divide dough into 12 large spoonfuls on prepared sheets and bake for 12–15 minutes or until scones are lightly golden.
7. Serve that day or allow scones to cool and wrap each individually in plastic wrap to keep fresh up to three days.

STRAWBERRY-RHUBARB BREAKFAST CRISP

GF, V	Serves: 8	Prep Time: 20 minutes	Bake Time: 50–55 minutes

Again: fruit, granola, topped with yogurt . . . totally breakfast.

- 2 pounds (roughly 5 cups) strawberries, sliced
- 2 pounds (8 cups) rhubarb, chopped
- 2/3 cup honey
- 6 tablespoons cornstarch
- 2 teaspoons vanilla extract
- 1 1/2 cups old-fashioned oats (gluten-free if needed)
- 1 1/2 cups almond flour
- 2/3 cup brown sugar
- 1/2 teaspoon salt
- 1/2 cup butter, melted
- 1/4 cup Greek yogurt, plus more for serving

1. Preheat oven to 350° F.
2. Mix together strawberries, rhubarb, honey, cornstarch, and vanilla extract. Spoon mixture into a large baking dish.
3. In a separate bowl, stir together oats, almond flour, brown sugar, and salt. Add Greek yogurt and melted butter. Stir well.
4. Spread the oat mixture over the strawberry-rhubarb filling.
5. Bake for 50–55 minutes. Serve warm, room temperature, or cold, with Greek yogurt.

POTATO & SWISS CRUSTLESS QUICHE

GF, V, NF	Serves: 8	Prep Time: 10 minutes (active), 8 hours (inactive)	Cook Time: 45 minutes

What's also easy enough to cook with a newborn baby strapped to your chest? This vegetarian version of the Ham & Cheddar Quiche. It too is crustless, which saves time and makes it an easy staple for gluten-free guests.

6 eggs
1 cup milk
1 cup grated Swiss cheese
1 large baking potato, peeled, halved lengthwise, and thinly sliced
3 tablespoons chives
1 teaspoon salt
freshly ground black pepper

1. Preheat oven to 350° F.
2. Lightly butter the bottom and sides of a 9-inch round pie pan.
3. Layer potatoes in the bottom of the pie pan.
4. In a separate bowl, whisk together the milk, eggs, cheese, salt, and pepper. Add chives and gently stir.
5. Pour egg mixture over the potatoes and either bake immediately or cover and refrigerate overnight.
6. Bake uncovered for about 35–45 minutes or until the center is set. Serve hot or at room temperature.

CHIA PUDDING PARFAITS

GF, DF, V, VG, NF	Serves: 8	Prep Time: 5 minutes	Cook Time: Overnight refrigeration

For years, I never knew what to serve vegans at brunch. Every breakfast recipe I had called for eggs or dairy. And since I'm not a baker—or at least an adventurous one—attempting to make homemade vegan baked goods has always intimidated me. On our honeymoon, however, Chris and I stayed at the most amazing bed-and-breakfast in Quebec City: Auberge J. A. Moisan. Housed over the oldest existing grocery store in North America, it features tiny but exquisitely decorated rooms and the most delicious breakfasts I've ever had. On our second morning there, chia pudding was on the menu. Our host, Clement, shared a few of the ingredients with me. I played around with the recipe to figure out the rest. This is my closest approximation to what we were served that morning. It has solved my dilemma of what to serve vegan friends for breakfast, but it's so tasty that our definitely non-vegan family eats it year round.

3/4 cup chia seeds
2 (15 ounce) cans of coconut milk
6 tablespoons maple syrup
2 teaspoons vanilla extract
4 cups fresh berries

1. In a medium-sized bowl, stir together chia seeds, coconut milk, syrup, and vanilla.
2. Spoon into small mason jars, jam jars, or juice cups, leaving room at the top for berries.
3. Cover with lids or plastic wrap and refrigerate overnight or for at least 8 hours.
4. In the morning, top with berries and serve.

GRANDMA MILLER'S PUMPKIN BREAD

DF, V, NF*	Makes 2 Loaves	Prep Time: 15 minutes	Cook Time: 90 minutes

Growing up, it wasn't Thanksgiving or Christmas without my Grandma Miller's pumpkin bread. It still isn't. But because in the twenty-first century, September through December is now pumpkin season, you don't have to wait for major holidays to make this tasty treat. Any old Sunday brunch will do.

- 3 1/2 cups flour
- 3 cups sugar
- 1/2 teaspoon baking powder
- 1 teaspoon baking soda
- 1 1/2 teaspoons salt
- 1 teaspoon ground cloves
- 1 teaspoon cinnamon
- 1 teaspoon nutmeg
- 2 cups or 1 (15 ounce) can pumpkin puree
- 1 cup melted butter or vegetable oil
- 1 cup water
- 4 eggs
- 2 cups walnuts, chopped (omit for nut-free option)

1. Preheat oven to 325° F.
2. Mix flour, baking powder, baking soda, salt, and spices.
3. In a separate bowl, mix eggs, sugar, butter, water, and pumpkin.
4. Add dry ingredients to wet ingredients. Fold in nuts, if adding.
5. Divide batter into two greased loaf pans and bake for 90 minutes or until a toothpick comes out clean.
6. Serve warm, room temperature, or cold—but always with ample amounts of butter.

HASH BROWN BREAKFAST CASSEROLE

GF*, NF	Serves 8	Prep Time: 40 minutes (plus 8 hours to chill)	Cook Time: 1 hour 15 minutes

In 2002, I was a first-year graduate student at Franciscan University and stuck in Steubenville with my roommates for Thanksgiving. To cheer ourselves up, we feasted the entire weekend. One of the best parts of the four-day feast was the sausage breakfast casserole I made for Sunday brunch. It was warm and hearty, savory and spicy, and, as one of my non-egg-loving roommates pronounced, "not too eggy!" Decades later, I'm still making that sausage and hash brown casserole on Thanksgiving weekend . . . and Christmas morning . . . and Easter morning . . . and for every mini-reunion I host for my grad school friends and our families.

- 4 tablespoons extra virgin olive oil
- 1 pound pork sausage, loose or with casings removed
- 1 small onion, chopped
- 2 garlic cloves, minced
- 2 1/2 cups cubed frozen hash brown potatoes, thawed
- 1/2 cup finely diced red bell pepper
- 5 eggs
- 2 cups shredded sharp cheddar cheese
- 1 3/4 cups whole milk
- 1 cup Bisquick (or gluten-free baking mix)
- 1/4 teaspoon salt
- 1/4 teaspoon pepper
- 1/4 teaspoon crushed red pepper flakes
- 2 cups sour cream
- 2 cups salsa verde

1. In a large frying pan, heat 2 tablespoons of olive oil. Add the sausage and cook over medium-high heat until no longer pink and the sausage is crumbly (approximately 7–10 minutes).
2. Add the onion and red pepper and cook until the onion is slightly browned (approximately 3–5 minutes). During the last minute of cooking, add garlic and red pepper flakes.
3. Drain the sausage and onion mixture on a plate lined with paper towels. Wipe the frying pan clean.
4. Add the remaining oil to the pan and heat until the oil is so hot a drop of water sizzles in it. Then cook the hash browns over medium-high heat until the potatoes are slightly brown and just beginning to crisp. Remove from heat.
5. In a large bowl, beat 5 eggs. Add the milk and cheese. Next, add the baking mix, salt, and pepper. Stir to combine.
6. To the same bowl, add the sausage, onion, hash browns, and red pepper. Stir well.

7. Pour the mixture into a greased 9 x 13-inch pan. Cover and chill in the refrigerator overnight (or for at least 8 hours).
8. In the morning, preheat the oven to 350° F. Bake casserole covered with foil for 45 minutes. Remove the foil and cook for 15–20 minutes more or until a toothpick comes out clean.
9. Let the casserole stand for 10 minutes, then serve, or cover with foil and keep warm in the oven until ready to eat. Top with sour cream and salsa verde.

Tip: When doubling the recipe, I use an 11 x 17-inch baking dish and cook the casserole, covered, for 1 hour and 15 minutes, then for an additional 15 minutes uncovered.

Door County Bloody Mary

We are not, in general, vodka drinkers. If I buy vodka, it's usually for vodka sauce. But Bloody Marys on Easter, Christmas, and during our annual week with my sisters in Door County, Wisconsin, are a Stimpson family tradition, and I don't like breaking with tradition.

2 ounces vodka
3 ounces tomato juice
3/4 ounce dill pickle juice
1/4 ounce lemon juice
2 teaspoons horseradish
2 dashes Worcestershire sauce
2 dashes tabasco sauce
1 pinch celery salt, plus more for the rim of the glass
1 pinch black pepper
Optional garnishes: green olives, dill pickle spears, celery, meat sticks, string cheese, etc.

1. Wet the rim of your glass with the outer edge of a lemon, then place upside down on a plate sprinkled with celery salt to coat the rim. Fill glass with ice.
2. Fill a shaker halfway with ice, then add vodka, tomato juice, pickle juice, horseradish, tabasco, Worcestershire sauce, tabasco sauce, celery salt, and pepper.
3. Shake while saying one Hail Mary and pour into glass. Garnish as liberally as you like.

OUR FAVORITE GRANOLA

GF, V, DF, VG	Serves 12	Prep Time: 10 minutes	Cook Time: 20 minutes

During the Great Shrinkflation of 2022, when the company that made our favorite store-bought granola began shrinking the amount of granola in the package (while still charging the same price), I decided to start making my own granola. It took a solid year of trying different combinations of sweeteners, oils, and bake times before I settled on what I thought was the perfect recipe. Today, I still think its the perfect recipe, as do Chris and the kids. We go through at least one batch of this weekly, and it is a go-to around here, not only for quick weekday breakfasts but also for snacking all day long.

- 8 cups old-fashioned oats (gluten-free if needed)
- 1 cup coconut oil
- 3/4 cup honey
- 1/4 cup maple syrup
- 2 teaspoons vanilla extract
- 2 teaspoons salt
- 1 teaspoon cinnamon
- 1 teaspoon pumpkin pie spice
- 2 cups pecan halves
- 1/2 cup raw pumpkin seeds
- 2 cups raisins

1. Preheat oven to 350° F and line a full baking sheet (or two half sheets) with parchment paper.
2. In a small saucepan, combine coconut oil, honey, maple syrup, and vanilla over low heat. Warm until melted. Stir in salt and spices and remove from heat.
3. In a large bowl, combine oats with melted oil and sugars. Stir well.
4. Spread granola evenly over pan and bake for 12 minutes. Remove from the oven and scatter pecans and pumpkin seeds across top.
5. Return granola to the oven and cook 7–10 minutes more, or until golden brown (my oven consistently wants seven minutes more).
6. Remove from oven, scatter raisins on top, and using a spatula, press granola firmly down onto the pan (this will help form clusters).
7. Allow the granola to cool for at least 20 minutes (the longer the wait, the bigger the clumps), then transfer to an airtight container.

INRI

TASTING HEAVEN

Food, the Eucharist, and Thursday Night Dinners

I know what I should remember most about my graduate school days at Franciscan University is what I learned in class. Memories of Dr. Scott Hahn telling the story of salvation history and Dr. Regis Martin waxing rhapsodic about Flannery O'Connor should fill my head. And they do . . . but only a corner of it. Most of my memories center on what happened outside the classroom, particularly on Thursday nights.

Every Thursday evening, I would wrap up my studies early and head downstairs to the kitchen in our little rental house on South Bend Boulevard. After pouring myself a glass of wine, I'd begin prepping my vegetables. Before long, a roommate would join me. Each week, one took a turn as my designated sous chef. As we chopped, stirred, and fried, we'd sing and dance around the kitchen, accompanied by Norah Jones, Over the Rhine, and, for some mysterious reason, Neil Diamond. His *Greatest Hits* CD was the sound of Summer 2004.

By 6:00 p.m., the other roommates would appear to set the table. Guests started arriving soon after. During the earliest days of our Thursday Night Dinners, those guests were mostly boyfriends and guy friends. I think we began the dinners to prevent them from showing up randomly during the week expecting food. Soon, though, we started to invite classmates, co-workers, and neighbors as well.

In the little South Bend Boulevard house, we squeezed just over a dozen people around our dining room table. By the time I'd finished school and purchased a home of my own, three blocks away, we abandoned the idea of eating at the table, and our numbers swelled to more than thirty. Once children began arriving (in a fast and furious fashion), we topped fifty on some nights.

Even as the locations changed and numbers grew, however, the heart of Thursday Night Dinners remained the same.

Dinner Time

First, there was the food: risotto with sausage and butternut squash, pierogies with spinach and cheese, curried couscous with pistachios and feta, Greek lasagna, tomato salad, sausage and kale soup, and brussels sprouts—so many brussels sprouts—roasted, with ample amounts of garlic and salt (and sometimes bacon). Each dish was as delicious and plentiful as I could make it. On Thursday nights, we ate and we ate well—student loans or not.

Along with the food came the wine, as most guests arrived with a bottle in hand. In the beginning, everyone brought the cheap stuff: $5 bottles of Moscato and $7 bottles of Yellow Tail Shiraz. With time, we switched to the good stuff: California Cabernets, French Bordeaux, and even the occasional White Burgundy. Good beer came as well. We drank it all, with those bottles doing exactly what Sirach said they would: help our hearts rejoice and make glad our souls (Sir 31:28).

Then, there was the conversation. Nothing was off limits. Henri de Lubac and Hans Kung, George Bush and Barack Obama, the Charismatic Movement and the Latin Mass, *Lost* and *American Idol,* breastfeeding, co-sleeping, homeschooling—all the usual Steubenville fare. Not surprisingly, debates raged late into the night. Voices were raised. But no serious damage was done.

Those Thursday Night Dinners, from first to last, are the best memory I have of my single years. Over shared plates of shepherd's pie, strangers became friends, and friends became family. As the years passed and we married off, one by one, people whom we'd never known before Thursday Night Dinner became our best men and maids of honor. When babies were born, we became godparents to each other's children (I have six Thursday Night Dinner godchildren and counting). We've also driven across the country to support each other at parents' funerals; lost sleep helping each other renovate houses; and prayed countless novenas for each other in times of crisis.

And we owe that, in large part, to food.

Cooking Lessons

Food—ample and good—gave us a reason to gather; it brought us together. Food nourished our bodies as the conversation that unfolded around it nourished our spirits. Food gave comfort to weary students worn out from grueling exams, and it gave strength to even wearier parents worn out from potty-training toddlers. The more babies were born, the more the moms loved answering their little ones' questions of "What's for dinner?" with "Whatever Emmie is making."

Food—ample and good—gave us a reason to gather; it brought us together. Food nourished our bodies as the conversation that unfolded around it nourished our spirits.

For me in particular, the food I cooked became a tangible way of showing my love for my friends. I spent countless hours in my Steubenville kitchens cooking up tasty things for them to eat. It cost me money and it cost me energy, but it was worth it. I wanted every bite of every meal to communicate to my friends that they were loved, that they mattered, and that they were worth every ounce of effort it took to chop those brussels sprouts and stir those risottos.

For all of us, Thursday Night Dinners offered not just an experience of community, but more fundamentally, an experience of communion, of the unity that comes from a shared life and shared purpose. As we partook of the same meal, we also partook of the same vision of the good life. Or, more accurately, we partook of the same vision of eternal life—of a Feast that never ends, of a Supper that satisfies completely, of a Banquet that nourishes, strengthens, comforts, and forges unbreakable bonds of spiritual friendship.

In other words, our Thursday Night Dinners, in their own imperfect way, foreshadowed the Marriage Supper of the Lamb . . . just as every meal should.

Reading the Recipe

As Christians, we know we live in a world of sacred signs. Everything bears the mark of its Creator. Every butterfly, every mountain, every sunset, reveals some truth about the One who made it. All Creation speaks of God, teaching us about his love, majesty, power, and mercy. Food is no exception. Brussels sprouts and broccoli stalks, crispy fried gnocchi, and hearty loaves of bread all point beyond themselves to something else: the Eucharist.

Everything food does on the natural level—nourish, strengthen, comfort, heal, and create community—the Eucharist does on the supernatural level. It nourishes, strengthens, comforts, and heals our souls with God's life, and as it does that, it builds the ultimate community: the Body of Christ.

Likewise, the sacrifice that goes into preparing supper for the ones we love hints at the sacrifice that God made to prepare the Supper upon which we feast every Sunday. Our generosity is a faint imitation of his radical generosity. We stand over a hot stove; he offered his life on the Cross.

Finally, just as the meals we serve demonstrate our love for the ones we serve, there is

no greater demonstration of God's love for us than the Eucharist. It is love that we can taste, see, and feel, love that makes itself vulnerable, and love that is never received with the gratitude it deserves.

What food ultimately offers us is a Eucharistic theology, a way of understanding what the Eucharist does in us and in the world. That theology comes straight from God himself. He cooked it up long ago. Before Adam fell, before Israel wandered, before the Word took on flesh, he designed food to teach us about his Eucharistic Self. Just as he did with all the rest of Creation, he wrote meaning into meals, crafting culinary signs and gastronomic symbols that would help us understand who he is and how very much he loves us.

As Paul explained to the Greeks of Lystra, "In past generations [God] allowed all the nations to walk in their own ways; yet he did not leave himself without witness, for he did good and gave you from heaven rains and fruitful seasons, satisfying your hearts with food and gladness" (Acts 14:16–17).

It didn't have to be that way. God could have designed our bodies to soak up nutrition from the sun and rain. He could have made us to be nourished by a singular plant—a superfood to beat all superfoods. He also could have made a sad, sad world where every ingredient tasted like beets. But he did not.

Instead, he made us to eat many things—tomatoes and avocados, strawberries and blueberries, bread and butter. He made lemons tart and pecans sweet. He made coffee invigorating and bacon magical. He imbued chocolate with the ability to strengthen our hearts and gave wine the power to lower our blood pressure. He then thought up brussels sprouts and inspired some culinary genius to roast them to crispy, caramelized perfection. He also thought up dozens of herbs and hundreds of spices, giving us the tools to imitate his creativity every time we enter a kitchen.

Then, to top it all off, God made us so that we needed to eat not just once, but three times daily, giving us the best possible excuse to stop all our busy "doing" and be with people we love, talking and laughing over shared bowls of macaroni and cheese.

All that is by design. None of it is coincidence. God does nothing randomly, least of all how he feeds us.

Giving Thanks

The year before I first came to Franciscan, shortly after I returned to the Catholic Church, I was walking back to my pew after Holy Communion and a thought came to me: The most intimate communion I have with God is that I eat him.

Over and over again those words ran through my head. I eat God. In the Eucharist, he becomes food for me. In the Eucharist, I take his life into me.

At the time, I was on the tail end of a six-year battle with anorexia, and that thought upended my world. It did what no amount of counseling or any support group could do. It brought clarity, grace, and profound healing, taking away my fear of food and replacing it with awe.

Despite this newfound understanding, though, when I arrived in Steubenville, just nine months later, I was still working out its practical implications.

And that brings us back to Thursday Night Dinners.

In those long, late, happy nights, theory and praxis fully became one. As my friends and I feasted, I saw the power of a pot of pumpkin soup to bless, comfort, heal, strengthen, gladden, and incarnate love. And as I saw all that, I finally stopped thinking of food in terms of fat grams and calories. I stopped weighing and measuring it out. Because you don't weigh and measure love—you lavish it on others and you receive it, gratefully, yourself.

You also don't abuse so great a gift; you don't eat it secretly, hastily, greedily, daintily, or gluttonously. You eat it reverently, taking neither too much nor too little, giving your body what it needs of both kale and salted caramel ice cream cake, so you can go about doing all the loving and serving God made you to do.

My friends often say that Thursday Night Dinners were one of the best gifts I've given them. Maybe. But they were definitely one of the best gifts God has given me. They helped me to approach every meal eucharistically—joyfully and gratefully. They also helped me to approach the Eucharist even more joyfully and gratefully, my understanding of it deepened by my deeper understanding of food. Over so many nights and so many years, those dinners showed me how to live this theology of food—to put it into practice. And I miss them.

Those Thursday Night Dinners came to an end when I married and left Steubenville for Pittsburgh. Most of the other regular dinner attendees moved as well. I'm back now, at long last, living with my husband and little ones just blocks from where all those dinners took place, but most everyone else is spread out across the country and makes their own dinners on Thursday nights. Even all these years later, though, when I walk into my kitchen on a Thursday night, I think about those grand old dinners. They offered to all of us a foretaste of the Wedding Supper that will never come to an end—of the Feast where every dish is better than the dish before, where everyone is perfectly satisfied, and where nobody needs to leave and go home . . . because we're already there.

Over so many nights and so many years, those dinners showed me how to live this theology of food—to put it into practice.

APPETIZERS

During my single years, I hosted an annual Christmas party, where dozens of friends and their many dozens of children came to my house to drink craft cocktails, eat fancy appetizers, and help me decorate my Christmas tree.

Also, when I was single, I thought every fancy dinner party needed to start with an appropriately fancy appetizer. So, over the course of fifteen years, I developed quite the roster of fancy appetizers to serve.

These days, with three small children racing (quite literally) around my kitchen, I'm no longer in the season of fancy anything. I'm more in the season of "Come hang out in my kitchen and drink wine while I cook and our children run feral." So, with few exceptions, fancy appetizers have fallen by the wayside. In their place, you'll usually find a big old plate of cheese and crackers.

When the season of fancy appetizers comes again, though, I'll look forward to plating all these up once more.

WHITE BEAN & BASIL HUMMUS

GF, V, NF	Serves 8	Prep Time: 10 minutes

My friend Tom calls this "green crack dip." Which it pretty much is; it's that addictive. We serve it either with pita chips, crackers, or crostini. I've also been known to eat it with a spoon.

- 1 (15 ounce) can cannellini beans, drained and rinsed
- 1 (15 ounce) can artichoke hearts, drained and rinsed
- 1 cup finely grated Parmesan cheese
- 1/2 cup chopped fresh basil
- 1 large lemon, zested and juiced
- 1 teaspoon salt
- 1/2 cup extra virgin olive oil

1. In a food processor, combine beans, artichoke hearts, cheese, basil, 1 teaspoon lemon zest, lemon juice, and salt.
2. Puree all ingredients together, slowly drizzling olive oil into the mixture until it is blended smooth.
3. Cover tightly with plastic wrap and refrigerate until time to serve (keeps fresh in the fridge for 4–6 hours). Stir immediately before serving.

BACON-WRAPPED DATES

GF, DF, NF	Yield: 32 pieces	Prep Time: 15 minutes	Cook Time: 40 minutes

There are about a hundred elaborate ways to cook bacon-wrapped dates. Mine are not elaborate. But if I didn't serve these on Christmas, most of my friends and family would turn around and leave.

I have not yet figured out a way to always have equal amounts of bacon and dates. Some of one is always left over. If you do figure it out, though, please let me know!

1 pound bacon
2 pounds pitted dates
toothpicks

1. Preheat oven to 375° F.
2. Line a large, rimmed baking sheet with parchment paper.
3. Slice the whole pound of bacon in half, horizontally.
4. Wrap each date in bacon, and stab through with toothpick, securing bacon.
5. Bake in oven, on parchment-lined baking sheet, until bacon crisps (about 40 minutes).
6. Serve immediately.

CRANBERRY CHUTNEY

GF, DF, V, VG, NF	Serves 8–10	Prep Time: 5 minutes	Cook Time: 30 minutes

Technically, this is a side dish for Thanksgiving. But I try not to get hung up on technicalities. It's just as good served over cream cheese for Christmas and New Year's parties, or as a dipping sauce for my Sausage and Cranberry Meatballs (see p. 48). For dairy-free guests, just set some of the chutney aside in a separate dish without cream cheese and serve with crackers.

- 2 cups (16 ounces) fresh cranberries
- 1 Granny Smith apple, peeled, cored, and chopped
- 1 1/4 cups sugar
- 3/4 cup water
- 2 teaspoons cinnamon
- 1 teaspoon ground ginger
- 1/4 teaspoon ground cloves

1. Combine all ingredients in a medium-sized saucepan and bring to a boil.
2. Reduce heat and simmer until mixture has thickened to a chutney consistency (about 30 minutes).
3. Cool, then refrigerate until ready to use.

Chatsworth
in 1792

1/2 tsp

GORGONZOLA TOASTS

V, NF	Yield: 20–25 pieces	Prep Time: 5 minutes	Bake Time: 8–10 minutes

Every once in a while, for an ordinary, run-of-the-mill, just-having-a-few-friends-over kind of dinner, I decide to set out something for guests besides meat, cheese, and olives. This, along with some wine, keeps them happy while I cook the rest of the meal.

half a baguette, sliced into 1/2-inch pieces
4 ounces crumbled Gorgonzola or blue cheese
extra virgin olive oil
honey

1. Preheat oven to 375° F.
2. Arrange bread on a sheet pan and brush liberally with olive oil.
3. Toast the bread in oven until it just begins to brown (about 5 minutes).
4. Remove bread from oven and sprinkle cheese evenly on top. Return to the oven and toast until cheese begins to melt (about 2–3 minutes).
5. Arrange on a platter, drizzle with honey, and serve.

APRICOT BITES

GF, V	Yield: 20 pieces	Prep Time: 10 minutes

If you want your dinner party to look fancy but, like me, don't have the time for fancy, these tasty bites are the way to go.

If you choose to make these ahead, pull the tray out of the fridge 15–20 minutes before serving to bring them to room temperature.

4 ounces goat cheese, softened
20 dried apricots
20 roasted almonds
honey

1. Spread a small amount of goat cheese on each apricot.
2. Place an almond in the center of each.
3. Arrange the fruit on platter and drizzle with honey.
4. Serve immediately or refrigerate, for up to 8 hours, until ready to serve.

HOT ARTICHOKE DIP

GF, V, NF	Serves 12	Prep Time: 5 minutes	Cook Time: 30 minutes

Two decades ago, I spent a year helping to run a Christian retreat house for political leaders. That was where I first learned how to cook, and this was the first appetizer I learned how to make. All these years later, I still make it. Partly because it's ridiculously easy. Partly because it's ridiculously tasty.

2 (15 ounce) cans artichoke hearts
2 cups mayonnaise
2 cups shredded Parmesan cheese

1. Preheat oven to 350° F.
2. In a food processor or powerful blender, puree all ingredients together.
3. Spread mixture into a 9-inch square (or similarly sized) baking dish and bake for 30 minutes.
4. Serve hot or cover with foil and keep warm until ready to eat. Serve with crackers or baguette slices.

SAUSAGE & CRANBERRY MEATBALLS

GF, NF	Yield: 24–30 pieces	Prep Time: 10 minutes	Cook Time: 20 minutes

This was one of my Christmas party staples. Now they're my go-to appetizer in the winter when someone asks me to bring one to a dinner or party. They come together quickly and keep warm for hours in a crockpot.

1 pound bulk sweet Italian sausage, loose or with casings removed

1/3 cup fresh cranberries, roughly chopped

1/2 cup grated Gruyère cheese

2 tablespoons minced shallots

2 garlic cloves, minced

1/2 cup instant or quick-cooking oats

1 teaspoon baking powder

1 teaspoon salt

1/8 teaspoon black pepper

1. Preheat oven to 350° F and line a rimmed baking sheet with parchment paper.
2. In a large mixing bowl, combine all ingredients and mix well (hands are better than a spoon for this).
3. Roll the mixture into balls and place on a baking sheet. Bake for 25 minutes.
4. Serve immediately (with cranberry chutney or cranberry sauce) or keep warm in a crockpot until ready to serve.

CORNED BEEF PICKLES

GF, NF	Yield: 3–4 dozen pieces	Prep Time: 20 minutes (active), 4 hours (inactive)

If you grew up anywhere in the Midwest, chances are your grandmother made these for Christmas, weddings, funerals, cookouts, and every other get-together in the calendar year. But unlike the Jell-O salads, this recipe is still good enough to make now, especially if salty snacks are your thing, like they are mine. If you can find it, use Buddig Corned Beef, which is sliced especially thin.

1 (32 ounce) jar whole dill pickles
1 cup (8 ounces) cream cheese, softened
4 ounces thinly sliced corned beef deli meat

1. Lay out 2 slices of corned beef. Arrange so they're large enough to wrap around the pickle.
2. Spread a generous layer (about 1 1/2–2 tablespoons) of cream cheese across the meat.
3. Wrap meat around the pickle.
4. Refrigerate for 4 hours.
5. Slice into half-inch disks and arrange on a platter.
6. Serve immediately or cover and refrigerate for 2–3 hours.

BACON-WRAPPED CAJUN-STUFFED PEPPERS

GF, NF	Yield: 40 peppers	Prep Time: 20 minutes	Cook Time: 20–30 minutes

My old garden in Steubenville grew an abundance of peppers. One summer, we harvested more than two thousand. I gave away as many as I could. Others we roasted with onions, threw in salsas, and chopped up for soups. The rest we wrapped in bacon and filled with spicy cream cheese, serving them at every dinner party, cookout, and happy hour we hosted that summer.

20 Hungarian wax peppers, halved and seeded

1 cup (8 ounces) cream cheese, softened

1 tablespoon Creole seasoning

20 slices of bacon, cut in half horizontally

toothpicks

1. Heat oven to 375° F.
2. In a small dish, combine Creole seasoning and cream cheese.
3. Using a small spoon or butter knife, fill each pepper half with the seasoned cream cheese. Wrap pepper halves with half a slice of bacon, and secure with a toothpick.
4. Place on a parchment-lined baking tray and bake for 20–30 minutes, or until bacon is completely cooked.
5. Serve immediately.

BURRATA CROSTINI WITH FRESH HERBS

V	Serves: 8	Prep Time: 10	Cook Time: 5 minutes

The garden in our Pittsburgh home was a much humbler thing than my first Steubenville garden. But what it unfailingly produced for us was herbs. This simple herb pesto, heaped on top of creamy burrata cheese and good bread, was my favorite way to put those herbs to use.

1/2 cup fresh basil

1/4 cup fresh dill

1/4 cup fresh mint

1 cup dry roasted cashews

4 tablespoons extra virgin olive oil, plus more for bread

8 ounces burrata

salt

8 thick slices of crusty bread

1. Finely chop herbs and place in a medium-sized bowl.
2. Roughly chop cashews and add to the herbs.
3. Drizzle olive oil into the herb and nut mixture. Toss to combine and salt to taste.
4. Drizzle bread with olive oil and toast in a toaster oven or toaster until golden.
5. Evenly divide burrata and spread across the bread. Top with herb and nut mixture, and serve immediately.

Chatsworth

PRACTICAL HOSPITALITY

How Clean Is Clean Enough?

Let's talk housekeeping. Not ordinary housekeeping. Not "Do the Laundry on Wednesdays and Clean the Bathrooms on Fridays" housekeeping. But, rather, "Friends Are Coming Over Tonight, and We Need to Get the House Ready" housekeeping. What exactly, in this scenario, does "get the house ready" mean?

This is a bad idea. If you think you need to deep clean your house every time friends come calling, you will either never have friends over or everyone in your family, including you, will dread it when you do.

That being said, we all want to honor our guests as best as we can, and sending them into a bathroom visibly frequented by a three-year-old boy in the middle of potty-training seems . . . well . . . less than honoring.

If you think you need to deep clean your house every time friends come calling, you will either never have friends over or everyone in your family, including you, will dread it when you do.

This is an important question, because how you answer it determines: 1) How free you feel to have people over for dinner; and 2) How crazy you make yourself and everyone in your household prior to your guests' arrival.

Over the years, many people I've talked to about this are under the impression that before anyone crosses the threshold of their homes, they must scrub their baseboards with a toothbrush.

So, when hosting, what do you need to do? What is the absolute minimum for pre-guest cleaning?

Here's how I answer that question in my own home, which, despite my best efforts, always looks like three very busy, very creative small children live in it.

Must Do (For Guests)

For the personal comfort and enjoyment of guests, I absolutely need to do only two (sometimes three) things before anyone arrives at my door for dinner.

- In the bathroom guests will use, I wipe down the toilet, sink, and the floor in front of the toilet (because of those aforementioned children). I might put out a fresh hand towel if necessary. If I think guests will use our upstairs hall bathroom in addition to the downstairs powder room, I do all that again upstairs.
- I clear off the dining room table and/or living room chairs, moving laundry, papers, books, etc. (even if that means just temporarily relocating them to a closet or bedroom). Because guests need a place to sit.
- If there is a crawling or toddling baby numbered among our guests, I clear the floor of any items on which they could possibly choke. I find having guests with babies over is the best possible excuse to relegate all Legos to the basement (where they are supposed to live but never really do).

Must Do (For Me)

Those three things are my absolute minimum. They're all I know I must do. And they're all I think anyone else must do either. But over the years, I have found that for my own sanity, doing a few more things helps if I have time.

- Clear kitchen counters of dirty dishes used earlier in the day (or week).
- Wash dirty dishes and run the dishwasher.
- Wipe down the kitchen counters.
- Sweep the kitchen floor.
- Straighten pillows in the living room and family room.
- Make our bed if it's not already made.

- Shut doors to any rooms I don't want people entering. (Will some people still enter those rooms? Possibly. Will their small children enter them? Likely, but this is what the Church calls an opportunity to cultivate detachment.)

Things I Do Not Worry About

Unless I'm hosting my husband's boss or a friend's wedding rehearsal dinner, there is a whole number of things I simply don't clean, such as

- Bedrooms: If they're messy, I close the door.
- Office: If it's messy (mine always is), I close the door.
- Bathrooms guests won't use: If they're messy, I close the door (you should be sensing a pattern here).
- Mudroom and laundry room: Despite what you see on Instagram, these are utility rooms, not show rooms; it's okay for them to look like what they are.
- Marks, handprints, and "artwork" on walls: I usually clean these things when I find them. But right before guests arrive is not the time to worry about this.
- Visible toys: If kids live in your house, you don't need to hide it. Just create a Lego-free path, move any large items that guests might trip over, and call it good.
- Dusting: You should dust your house from time to time, but dust bunnies won't kill anyone (unless they have a deadly dust mite allergy. Then maybe you should dust).
- Mopping.
- Windows: Just in case anyone is crazy enough to think cleaning windows is a necessary part of pre-hosting prep . . . it's not.

No matter what your mother may have thought, healthy human beings don't go to their friends' houses to see picture perfect homes and eat five-star cuisine. We have Instagram and restaurants for those things. Rather, we go to our friends' houses to be with our friends—to talk with them, laugh with them, and love them. And your ability to give that to people does not depend on your housekeeping skills. It depends on your willingness to let people into your home, be real with them, and love them where they are.

> ***But when in doubt, put yourself in your guests' shoes.***

So adapt my lists as you see fit. Some of you may need to do more for your sanity; others will do less. But when in doubt, put yourself in your guests' shoes. Think about what you really care about when you go somewhere for dinner. Then let the rest go.

SALADS

In college, when I struggled with anorexia, I subsisted for the better part of three years on salads made of iceberg lettuce, tuna, and Mrs. Dash. I don't recommend it.

Those salads were . . . lacking in so many ways.

Not the salads I'm sharing here. Most are densely packed with nutrients and far tastier than my college cafeteria concoctions of old. The majority are also easy to make ahead and work well for lunches when hosting houseguests or throwing summer cookouts.

Most also transport well and are healthier alternatives to baked pasta when new babies make an appearance and their moms need a meal brought to them.

Last, the number of servings indicated for each recipe is based on side salad portions unless otherwise noted.

ROSEMARY ALMOND CHICKEN SALAD

GF	Serves 12 (as a main course)	Prep Time: 30 minutes

Okay, so this particular salad is not what I would call "light." But it is, hands down, the single most requested lunch from my friends (and especially my friends' husbands), when they travel to stay at "Emily's B&B." You can poach, bake, or grill the chicken (I usually poach it) and serve the salad on bread or over lettuce. If you can, use a good quality mayonnaise—I prefer Sir Kensington's Avocado Oil Mayonnaise. This salad also keeps well in the refrigerator for several days, so if you have a baby in the summer, this is what I'll probably bring to your house when it's my turn to make you a meal.

- 4 pounds chicken breast, cooked
- 3 cups mayonnaise
- 1 1/2 cups (12 ounces) dried cherries
- 3 cups (12 ounces) slivered almonds
- about 1/4 cup (4–6 large sprigs) fresh rosemary leaves, removed from stems and chopped
- 1/2 cup sugar
- salt and pepper to taste

1. Cook chicken according to preferred method. Refrigerate until ready to use.
2. Dice cooked chicken into 1/2-inch pieces or shred in food processor or stand mixer.
3. In a large bowl, combine all ingredients. Salt and pepper to taste.
4. Refrigerate until ready to serve.

KALE & AVOCADO POWER SALAD

GF, DF, V	Serves: 18	Prep Time: 20 minutes

This is a crazy easy, crazy healthy, and crazy tasty salad to throw together for a cookout. Especially when your guest list is packed with gluten-free vegetarians.

To prepare for a crowd, boil and peel the eggs well ahead of time, then throw together the rest of the salad 10–15 minutes before eating.

12 eggs, hard or medium boiled (according to your preference), peeled, and sliced

3 avocados, peeled and sliced

1 1/2 cups walnuts, chopped

6 tablespoons roasted sunflower seeds

6 cups baby kale

6 cups arugula or mixed greens

extra virgin olive oil

salt and pepper to taste

1. In a large bowl, top greens with sunflower seeds, walnuts, eggs, and avocado slices.
2. Drizzle liberally with olive oil and sprinkle with salt and pepper. Toss to combine.

SWEET & SAVORY QUINOA SALAD

GF, DG, V, Vegan	Serves 15	Prep Time: 20 minutes	Cook Time: 5 minutes

When Chris and I were dating, he was recovering from some serious health issues. So my choleric self went on the hunt for healthy salads that he could take to work for lunch. This recipe, adapted from Whole Foods' California Salad, fit the bill. It makes a ton and keeps well in the fridge, so you can make it on Sunday, divide it up into little mason jars, and not worry about lunch until the following Sunday.

2 cups uncooked quinoa
3 2/3 cups vegetable broth
2 1/2 cups shelled edamame
1 cup chopped walnuts
1 cup slivered almonds
2 cups unsweetened shredded coconut
2 cups golden raisins
1 bunch cilantro (or parsley), chopped
1 medium red bell pepper, diced
1 medium red onion, diced
1 mango, peeled and diced
5 lemons, juiced
3 tablespoons white wine vinegar
2 teaspoons salt

1. Measure out quinoa into a mesh strainer. Rinse well and allow to drain.
2. Combine quinoa and broth in a medium-sized stockpot and bring to a boil. Reduce the heat, cover, and simmer for 15 minutes or until all the liquid is absorbed. (Alternately, combine the quinoa and broth in a rice cooker and cook on the white rice setting.)
3. When the quinoa is done, transfer to a large (very large) bowl, fluff with a fork, and allow it to cool for 5 minutes.
4. Combine all remaining ingredients in the bowl and mix well.
5. Refrigerate until ready to serve, as this tastes best cold.

CAPRESE PASTA SALAD

V, NF	Serves 8–10	Prep Time: 10 minutes	Cook Time: 10 minutes

This is another one of my favorite summertime meals to take to new moms. It doesn't need to be heated, keeps well in the fridge for days, and generally pleases the kids—as well as Mom and Dad. Use feta in brine if you can find it, as it's much creamier than other kinds.

- 1 pound penne or rigatoni pasta
- 16 ounces fresh mozzarella cheese, cubed into 1-inch chunks
- 4 ounces feta cheese, cubed into 1-inch chunks
- 4 vine-ripened tomatoes, chopped and drained of excess juices
- 1/2 cup roughly chopped fresh basil
- 1/2 cup extra virgin olive oil
- salt and pepper to taste

1. Bring a large pot of salted water to boil. Add pasta and cook until al dente. Drain and run under cold water to cool.
2. In a large bowl, combine the pasta, tomatoes, olive oil, and basil. Toss to coat.
3. To the same bowl, add cheeses and gently toss.
4. Season with salt and pepper to taste.
5. Refrigerate until ready to serve (or drop off at a new mom's house).

GREEN GODDESS BOWL

GF, V, NF	Serves: 8	Prep Time: 15 minutes	Cook Time: 30 minutes

If you're ever in Pittsburgh, one of the best places to grab a burger is a small local chain called Burgatory. Yes, it's a play on Purgatory, and the restaurant's slogan is "Heavenly Shakes, Helluva Burger." If you don't mind the irreverence, the burgers truly are fantastic. My favorite item on the menu, however, is not any of the burgers. Rather, it's their Green Goddess Bowl. This recipe is my own copycat version, and it's as close to the real thing as humanly possible. It's also a lot easier on our family budget than going to Burgatory.

To make this salad more substantial, I recommend topping with grilled chicken or a burger, but it's also a great vegetarian summer meal on its own (or a delicious side dish for a cookout).

- 2 cups uncooked quinoa
- 3 2/3 cups vegetable broth
- 3 sweet potatoes, peeled and diced
- 3 (15 ounce) cans chickpeas, drained and rinsed
- 4 ears fresh corn (or 32 ounces frozen corn)
- 1 large red onion, sliced
- 8 ounces feta cheese, preferably in brine
- 2 cups fresh parsley (leaves and stems)
- 1/4 cup fresh basil
- 1 clove garlic
- 12 anchovies packed in oil
- 2 teaspoons Dijon mustard
- extra virgin olive oil
- 1 cup white vinegar
- 1 cup sugar
- 1 cup water
- salt and pepper to taste

1. Preheat oven to 425° F.
2. Using a fine mesh strainer, thoroughly rinse quinoa. In a medium-sized pot, combine quinoa and broth. Bring to a boil, then reduce heat, cover, and allow to simmer for 15 minutes or until all the liquid is absorbed. Fluff cooked quinoa with a fork and set aside.
3. Meanwhile, peel and small dice sweet potato. Slice red onions. Remove the corn kernels from the ears (if using fresh corn). Drain chickpeas and dry thoroughly between paper towels (discarding any skins that come off).
4. Arrange sweet potatoes on one parchment-lined baking sheet. Drizzle them with oil and season with salt and pepper. On another parchment-lined sheet pan, arrange chickpeas and corn, then drizzle with olive oil and season with salt. Roast vegetables in the oven for 20–25 minutes, until chickpeas are crispy, corn is slightly blackened, and potatoes have started to caramelize.

(continued on next page ⇨)

5. While the vegetables roast, pickle your onions: Thinly slice onion and stuff slices into a pint-sized mason jar. In a small pot, combine vinegar and sugar with 1 cup of water and a pinch of salt. Heat until sugar is completely dissolved, then pour the liquid over the onions and seal the jar. Set aside.
6. As the veggies continue roasting, make the dressing. In a food processor, combine parsley, basil, garlic, anchovies, and mustard. Pulse until combined, then slowly drizzle in olive oil (about 1/4 cup) until the dressing is smooth and creamy.
7. In a large serving bowl, combine quinoa, sweet potatoes, chickpeas, and corn. Stir in the dressing gently, until combined, and top the salad with pickled red onions and feta, then serve.

Chris's Classic Dirty Dry Martini

This is my husband's signature drink. Dirty. Dry. Ice cold. It pairs wonderfully with grilled meats, Indian food, risotto, and toddlers.

With dirty martinis, you want to avoid gins that are heavy on botanicals. Our favorites for martinis are Hendricks, Bombay Sapphire, and Beefeater. The Botanist and Aviation also work well.

- 2 ounces gin
- a splash (about a teaspoon) of dry vermouth
- 2 tablespoons olive juice
- 3 large green olives, preferably garlic-stuffed

1. At least 5 minutes before making, stick a martini glass in the freezer. The secret to a good martini, truly, is an ice-cold glass.
2. Remove the glass from the freezer and add vermouth, swirling around until all the sides are coated.
3. Fill a shaker halfway with ice. Add gin and shake while saying one Hail Mary.
4. Pour into the martini glass. Add olive juice to taste, then garnish with olives.

HERBED POTATO SALAD

GF, DF, V, VG, NF	Serves 10–12	Prep Time: 15 minutes	Cook Time: 15 minutes

Back in the day before dairy allergies (remember those days?), the recipe for my Red Potato Salad (see p. 87) was all I needed for summer picnics. These days, I need other options, and this one is an excellent alternative.

- 4 pounds fingerling potatoes
- 1 bunch green onions, chopped
- 1/4 cup chopped fresh parsley
- 1/2 cup chopped fresh basil
- 1/4 cup chopped fresh dill
- 6 tablespoons white wine
- 6 tablespoons white vinegar
- 1/4 cup extra virgin olive oil
- 2 teaspoons Dijon mustard
- 3 garlic cloves, minced
- 4 teaspoons salt
- 1 1/2 teaspoons black pepper

1. Bring a large pot of salted water to boil. Add potatoes and boil until soft (15–20 minutes). Drain cooked potatoes and set aside in a large bowl to cool.
2. Meanwhile, chop herbs and garlic.
3. In a small bowl, combine wine, vinegar, oil, mustard, garlic, salt, and pepper and mix well.
4. Pour dressing over potatoes and gently mix in herbs. Check for salt and pepper and serve at room temperature.

ROASTED WINTER SALAD

GF, DF*, NF	Serves 8 (as a main course)	Prep Time: 15 Minutes	Cook Time: 35 Minutes

This is a favorite winter salad, which we serve as a main course with crusty bread and (sometimes) a bowl of soup. You can chop all the vegetables before guests arrive, cook the bacon and onion up to an hour before serving, and then just pop the vegetables in the oven 40 minutes before eating. While they cook, you can open the doors to your guests, drink wine, eat cheese, and chat. Then, pull the vegetables out of the oven, throw everything together in a large bowl, and sit down to dinner with your friends.

3 pounds potatoes
4 cups green beans, ends trimmed
2 large onions, thinly sliced
1 pound bacon
8 cups baby kale
8 cups baby spinach
extra virgin olive oil
3 tablespoons butter
10 garlic cloves, peeled and crushed
1 cup finely shredded pecorino-Romano or Parmesan cheese (omit for dairy-free option)
salt and pepper to taste

1. Preheat oven to 400° F. Wash and chop all vegetables, then set aside. If chopping potatoes more than 15 minutes in advance of cooking, place them in a bowl and cover with water.
2. Cook bacon until it has reached your desired level of crispiness then place it on a paper towel-lined plate and cover with foil to keep warm for up to one hour. Reserve 1 tablespoon of bacon fat.
3. Heat the reserved bacon fat and butter (or oil, for dairy-free option) in a frying pan. Add onion slices and turn the heat down to low. Allow the onions to caramelize, stirring frequently. It should take about 20 minutes. Remove the onions from heat and cover to keep warm.
4. In a large mixing bowl, toss potato pieces with 2 tablespoons of oil, 3 garlic cloves, 2 pinches of salt, and a smattering of pepper. Scatter onto a parchment-lined baking sheet and bake for 35 minutes or until potatoes are crisp and golden. Toss occasionally as they begin to brown.
5. While potatoes cook, in a mixing bowl, toss the beans, remaining garlic, 1 tablespoon of oil, one pinch of salt, and a smattering of pepper. Place on a parchment-lined sheet pan.
6. After the potatoes have cooked for 15–20 minutes, add green beans to oven and cook for 15–20 minutes more (until green beans are browned).
7. When the vegetables are done, immediately before eating, assemble the salad. Toss the greens with the roasted veggies, bacon, and onion. Drizzle with olive oil, salt to taste, and top with freshly grated cheese. Toss again and serve.

GREEK ORZO & CHICKEN SALAD

NF	Serves 6–8 (as a main course)	Prep Time: 15 minutes	Cook Time: 25 minutes

Years ago, when I lived in Washington, DC, my favorite place to go for lunch with coworkers was a little café in Union Station. I always ordered the same thing: Greek Orzo & Chicken Salad. When I moved to Steubenville, recreating it was my life's mission. This is as close as I managed to get. It's best served cold but tastes good warm too.

1 pound orzo pasta

4 chicken breasts, grilled or pan-fried and thinly sliced

2 cups (16 ounces) grape tomatoes, halved

1 (15 ounce) can black olives, sliced

4 sprigs fresh rosemary

1 tablespoon Cavender's All-Purpose Greek Seasoning (plus more to taste)

4 ounces feta cheese, crumbled

salt and pepper to taste

1/2 cup extra virgin olive oil

4 cups baby spinach

1. Bring a large pot of salted water to boil. Add orzo and cook until al dente. Drain pasta and run under water to cool. Set aside.
2. While the orzo boils, prep vegetables and remove rosemary leaves from stem, then roughly chop.
3. In a large bowl, combine orzo, chicken, olives, and tomatoes with olive oil, rosemary, and Greek seasoning. Add more seasoning and salt and pepper to taste and refrigerate until ready to serve.
4. Immediately before serving, divide spinach onto plates, top with orzo salad mixture and feta. Drizzle with more olive oil and serve.

FARRO & HERB SALAD

V, NF	Serves: 6–8	Prep Time: 40 Minutes

My new favorite summer salad is a twist on an old summer favorite, punched up with more herbs and flavor. If you don't like these particular herbs, just throw in the ones you do.

1 1/2 cups uncooked farro

4 cups water

4 tomatoes, chopped

1 (15 ounce) can chickpeas, rinsed and drained

1/4 cup finely minced chives

1/4 cup chopped Italian parsley

1/4 cup chopped basil

1/4 cup chopped dill

1 small yellow or red onion, minced

1/4 cup extra virgin olive oil

1 large lemon, seeded and juiced

2 garlic cloves, minced

8 ounces feta cheese, crumbled

salt and pepper to taste

1. Combine farro, water, and 2 tablespoons salt in a large pot. Bring to a boil, then reduce heat to low, cover, and simmer until tender (about 30 minutes). Drain and cool.
2. While the farro cooks, chop your tomatoes, onion, and herbs. Set aside in a large bowl.
3. Whisk together the oil, lemon juice, and garlic. Add salt and pepper to taste.
4. Combine the farro, tomatoes, onion, herbs, dressing, and feta.
5. Chill or serve at room temperature.

SUMMER CHOPPED SALAD

GF, DF, NF, V, VG	Serves 6	Prep Time: 10 minutes

This is one of my go-to weeknight side dishes in the summer. It takes just a few minutes to chop the veggies and pairs well with grilled meats, burgers, and pasta. My three-year-old, strange veggie-loving child that she is, has been known to have three helpings of it in one sitting.

2 cups (16 ounces) cherry tomatoes, halved

1 English cucumber, quartered and sliced

1/2 small red onion, diced

2 avocados, diced

1 (15 ounce) can chickpeas, rinsed and drained

2 tablespoons chopped fresh mint

1 medium lemon, juiced

1/4 cup extra virgin olive oil

salt and pepper to taste

1. Wash and prep all the vegetables, then toss them together in a large salad bowl.
2. In a small bowl, mix together lemon juice and olive oil. Add salt and pepper to taste.
3. Drizzle vegetables with dressing and toss to coat. Add a bit more olive oil if the vegetables are not evenly coated.
4. Add more salt and pepper to taste, and serve.

PESTO CHICKEN SALAD

Serves 6 (as a main course)	Prep time: 20 minutes	Cook Time: 10 minutes

Our new home in Steubenville was built in 1901 and looks like it belongs somewhere in the English countryside. It is fantastic in many ways but also lacks a few modern conveniences—for example, air conditioning. The absence of central air would be no big deal if we did, indeed, live in rural England. In Ohio in July, however, it is downright miserable. During the summer months, I try not to add to the misery by turning the oven on in the afternoon, which means salads like this one are on the menu most nights of the week.

3 (15 ounce) cans cannellini beans, drained and rinsed

3/4 cup pesto (I prefer DeLallo Simply Pesto)

1 small red onion, diced

2 tablespoons capers

1 cup pistachios, chopped

4 ounces feta cheese, crumbled

2 large or 3 medium lemons, zested and juiced

extra virgin olive oil

6 cups mixed greens (like arugula and spinach)

2 pounds chicken breasts, cut into bite-sized pieces

salt and pepper to taste

1. Prep vegetables in a large bowl by tossing together beans, pesto, red onion, and capers with the juice and zest of the lemons, then refrigerate.
2. While the salad chills, cook your chicken: pat chicken dry with paper towels. Season with salt and pepper. In a large frying pan, heat 2 tablespoons of olive oil until a drop of water sizzles in the pan. Add chicken and cook without stirring for 3–4 minutes or until browned. Toss and continue cooking until all chicken is browned and cooked through (about 7 minutes).
3. Remove the bean salad from the refrigerator. Toss in feta, chicken, and pistachios.
4. Fill a large salad bowl with greens. Top with beans and chicken and drizzle with olive oil. Check to see if additional salt and pepper are needed, and serve.

ITALIAN TUNA SALAD

GF, NF	Serves 6 (as a main course)	Prep Time: 20 minutes

Years ago, the television in our family room was left on after Daniel Tiger *ended, and when I went in to turn it off, I saw someone on PBS making this salad. That night, I put all the ingredients I could remember on my grocery list and made it for lunch the next day. Since then, I've tweaked and adjusted the recipe to make it extra filling and a little more child-friendly. The kids love it as much as I do, although when I serve it to them, I make sure our protein-loving Toby gets more tuna and chickpeas than celery, our fruit-loving Becket gets more grapes than celery, and our veggie-loving Ellie gets plenty of olives, celery, and red onion. Chris and I happily eat it all.*

6 eggs

3 (15 ounce) cans chickpeas, drained and rinsed

3 (5 ounce) cans oil-packed tuna

1 large red onion, sliced

6 celery stalks, sliced

3 cups red grapes, halved lengthwise or quartered

1 1/2 cups Castelvetrano olives, pitted and halved lengthwise

2 lemons, juiced

2 tablespoons capers

1/2 cup extra virgin olive oil

salt and pepper to taste

1. In a small saucepan, cover eggs with water. Bring to a boil, then cover and remove from heat. Let the pan sit for 10 minutes. Remove to a bowl of ice water to stop the cooking process. Peel under running water, quarter, and set aside.
2. In a small bowl, combine lemon juice and olive oil and whisk until combined. Add salt and pepper to taste.
3. In a large serving bowl, combine chickpeas, tuna, onion, celery, grapes, olives, and capers.
4. Slowly drizzle in lemon oil dressing and toss to combine. Taste and add more salt and pepper if desired.
5. Add eggs just before serving.

BURRATA WITH PROSCIUTTO & MELON

NF, GF	Serves 6	Prep Time: 5 minutes

In the summer of 2024, right before I before I began working on this new edition of the cookbook, Chris, the kids, and I led a pilgrimage to Italy. There we spent two glorious weeks exploring some of our favorite cities and churches in the world. We also spent two glorious weeks eating some of the best food in the world, including a salad very much like this one. Once we returned home, I began recreating it in my own kitchen, making it almost weekly for most of the summer.

1 large cantaloupe, peeled, seeded, and cut into bite-sized pieces

8 ounces burrata, torn into pieces

4 ounces prosciutto, torn into pieces

1 cup fresh basil leaves, loosely packed

3 tablespoons balsamic vinegar

1/4 cup extra virgin olive oil

salt and pepper to taste

1. Whisk together olive oil and vinegar. Season with salt and pepper to taste.
2. In a large serving bowl, combine cantaloupe, prosciutto, and basil. Add in burrata, then drizzle with dressing.
3. Serve chilled.

SALMON & WHITE BEAN SALAD

GF, NF	Serves 6 (as a main course)	Prep Time: 15 minutes	Cook Time: 60 minutes

When putting this new version of the cookbook together, I knew I wanted to include this salad, which is one of my favorite dinners to serve guests during the summer. I just wasn't sure where to put it. Should it go with the entrées or the salads? Because it is literally a salad, I settled on here. But make no mistake: it is elegant, delicious, and absolutely worthy of being the main course at a fancy dinner party.

The prep takes a bit of planning, although it's easier if you have two ovens or even an air fryer. I wrote out the instructions assuming most people have only one oven, but when I make it, I cook the potatoes in the air fryer while I am cooking the salmon in the oven. That makes things go a bit faster and keeps it all a bit simpler.

- 3 pounds salmon
- 1/4 cup chopped basil
- 1/4 cup chopped Italian parsley
- 1/4 cup chopped dill
- 3 (15 ounce) cans cannellini beans, drained and rinsed
- 6 large baking potatoes
- 1 large red onion, sliced
- 2–3 heads butter lettuce, washed and roughly chopped
- 1/2 cup mayonnaise
- 3 lemons
- 2 tablespoons capers
- 1/4 cup extra virgin olive oil, plus more for salmon
- 3 garlic cloves, minced
- salt and pepper to taste

1. Preheat oven to 375° F.
2. Chop herbs and thinly slice 1 and 1/2 lemons. In another bowl, mix together basil, dill, and parsley.
3. Pat salmon dry and season with salt and pepper, then transfer to a baking sheet lined with parchment. Drizzle the salmon with oil and then cover with herbs and lemon slices. Bake for 20–30 minutes (the thinner the salmon the more quickly it cooks) or until salmon easily flakes and reaches an internal temperature of 125°. Remove from the oven and allow it to rest, covering with foil to keep warm, if desired.

(continued on next page ⇨)

4. While the salmon bakes, bring a large pot of salted water to a boil. Peel potatoes and slice into 1-inch rounds. When the water comes to a boil, add the potatoes and cook for about 10 minutes. Drain then arrange on another parchment-lined sheet pan and drizzle with oil, seasoning generously with salt and pepper.
5. When the salmon has finished baking, increase the oven temperature to 500° F, roast the potatoes for 25 minutes (or until golden), and remove from the oven.
6. While the potatoes roast, make the dressing: mix together mayonnaise, the juice of 1 1/2 lemons, minced garlic, capers, and about a 1/4 cup of olive oil. Season with salt and pepper to taste.
7. To assemble the salad, toss together lettuce, beans, onion, and dressing in a large serving bowl, top with salmon and potatoes and serve immediately.

South Side

If you're looking to toast to the pope's health, here is our go-to drink. Rumor has it that it takes its name from Pope Leo XIV's childhood neighborhood in Chicago. I have not confirmed this. But I have confirmed that it's a fantastic summer drink, similar to a French 75 but without the pricey champagne. I like mine on the tart side, but feel free to add 1/2 ounce more of simple syrup if you like your drinks sweeter.

- 6 mint leaves
- 1 ounce freshly squeezed lemon juice
- 2 ounces gin
- 1/2 ounce simple syrup

1. Place 5 mint leaves and lemon juice in a cocktail shaker. Gently muddle. Add ice to the shaker, filling halfway. Add gin and simple syrup. Shake vigorously for the length of time it takes to pray one Hail Mary. Pour into an ice-cold glass and garnish with mint.

RED POTATO SALAD

GF, NF, V	Serves: 8–10	Prep Time: 15 minutes	Cook Time: 15 minutes

I have never been a mustard and mayonnaise potato salad kind of girl. Mustard, I like. Mayonnaise, I like. Mustard and mayonnaise in potato salad? Not so much. But this potato salad? This I love.

5 pounds red potatoes, cut into quarters (or into 6–8 pieces, if potatoes are very large)

1 cup plain whole milk yogurt

1 cup sour cream

1 pound bacon

1 bunch green onions, chopped

1/2 tablespoon Lawry's Seasoned Salt (plus more to taste)

1. Bring a large pot of salted water to boil and boil chopped potatoes until soft (15–20 minutes). Drain and cool.
2. While the potatoes boil, cook bacon until crisp. Drain off grease and chop the bacon into bite-sized pieces.
3. In a small bowl, whisk together yogurt, sour cream, and Lowry's Seasoned Salt.
4. In a large bowl, mix potatoes, yogurt dressing, bacon, and green onions. Check for taste, adding more seasoned salt if desired (I usually add a little more, but I tend to like this on the salty side).

PRACTICAL HOSPITALITY

The Guest on the Special Diet

Everyone has one: The friend who's gone Paleo. The son-in-law who won't touch animal products. The co-worker who swore off nightshade vegetables, soy lecithin, and foods that start with the letter "B."

Feeding any one of those people can be a challenge—especially when you have no idea what qualifies as a "nightshade vegetable." Feeding all three of them together at a dinner party is enough to make any sane person swear off entertaining for good.

It didn't use to be this way. Once upon a time—like ten years ago—you could invite a gaggle of friends over for dinner and feel reasonably certain they would all eat the spaghetti and meatballs you put before them. Back then, throwing a dinner party in no way resembled an episode of *Iron Chef*. Now, it does. So what's a good hostess to do? To what extent do we try to accommodate everyone's different and special diets?

Speaking only for my less-than-saintly self, here's how I handle guests with special dietary needs.

First, I try to remember my primary responsibility as a hostess: to love and honor my guests.

On the one hand, loving and honoring my guests means serving them a tasty meal that doesn't send them into anaphylactic shock or leave them doubled over in pain for the rest of the night. It also means doing my best to feed them food they can eat and will enjoy.

On the other hand, loving and honoring my guests means being kind, attentive, and calm—something I can't do if I've had to prepare six separate dishes for six different diets (and spend the entire month's grocery budget in the process).

First, I try to remember my primary responsibility as a hostess: to love and honor my guests.

So with that in mind, I make distinctions, assigning guests' dietary needs to various categories.

- Category One includes people with deadly airborne food allergies. I'm not talking about sensitivities here—like "sugar makes me grumpy." I'm talking about, "If I eat almonds, smell almonds, or inhale almond dust, I will stop breathing."
- Category Two consists of guests with food allergies or sensitivities that aren't airborne. For example, someone who has a wheat intolerance or is diabetic. They're not going to drop dead from being in the same room as a piece of bread, but a table full of pasta, bread, and cookies probably won't help them feel the love.
- Category Three includes people who are on "a diet." These guests need to lose a few pounds and have concluded that the way to do that is to never eat bread again. Or bacon. Or cream. They don't have an actual medical problem with any particular food. They just want to lose some weight.
- Category Four is the catchall for any remaining food issues: the vegetarians, the vegans, the Paleos, the macrobiotic raw foodies, and the just plain picky crowd. The common denominator in this category is choice. They may have good reasons for that choice (they're fighting cancer and hope a vegan diet will help); they may have silly reasons (Gwyneth Paltrow said to do it). But certain death has not forced them into this particular dietary habit.

Once I've placed my guests into their categories, I move on to the next step: meal planning. So which needs do I accommodate?

Obviously, if there are people coming over to the house who fall into Category One—deadly allergies—I must accommodate them. Always. There should not be a nut or a shellfish or something equally deadly anywhere in sight. Because . . . well . . . death.

The second category is also a no-brainer. People with celiac disease may not drop dead on the spot if there's bread on the table, but they're not just inventing this problem either. So if someone with a serious food allergy or sensitivity is coming over for dinner, I plan a meal that won't result in them spending the night on the bathroom floor. I also take whatever precautions necessary to prevent cross-contamination. Cooking polenta instead of pasta is easy enough. And the stress of putting together a menu that doesn't make my guests sick is way less than the stress of sending my guests to the hospital.

Once we get to the third category—dieters—I'm less accommodating. If only one person is coming to my house for dinner and they opt to follow some kind of fad diet, I will do my best to cook something they can eat. Again, I want my guests to be happy. But if I am cooking for many people and one of those other people has a real dietary restriction, the person on the weight loss diet is just going to have to deal. When I'm busy trying to make sure nobody is dying at my table, there's no time to worry if the protein-to-fat ratio in the dinner is sufficient to keep someone in ketosis. The dieter can just take a smaller helping of stew and skip the bread.

And what about the rest? The vegans? The carnivores? The Paleos? I accommodate them as much as possible. Like with the dieters, if it's they and only they who are coming over for dinner, I make a meal that meets their needs. And if I'm feeding a crowd, I will try to make sure there is something on the table they can eat. But if for some reason I can't do that or if there is an over-abundance of people with special dietary needs coming to a party, I'll ask the particular guest to bring a dish they like. I have yet to have a guest fail to understand that request, and most comply happily.

> ***The stress of putting together a menu that doesn't make my guests sick is way less than the stress of sending my guests to the hospital.***

All this, of course, presupposes one's guests actually announcing before they arrive that, for example, they avoid meat on principle. I've made it a habit to ask about food issues before I meal plan for guests, but if I ask and they keep quiet about their issue until dinnertime . . . well, that's what GrubHub is for, I guess.

SOUPS

When I feed a crowd, soups are one of my favorite, low fuss, low muss meals. I can do all the work well before guests arrive and have the kitchen completely clean to boot.

When I'm feeding our family on a weeknight, soups are also one of my favorite meals. They are, without fail, the one thing all my children love to eat.

Either way, pair any of these soups with a simple salad and bread and you have the makings of a wonderful dinner . . . for thirty or for five.

SAUSAGE, KALE & TOMATO SOUP

GF, DF*, NF	Serves 6–8	Prep Time: 15 minutes	Cook Time: 45 minutes

I've shared this soup on my old blog. I've shared this soup in The Catholic Table *book. I've shared this soup in* The Catholic Table *video series. And I will go on sharing this soup everywhere I can until I die because if you don't have this soup in your fall/winter dinner rotation, you are not living your best life.*

Now that I am cooking this regularly for small children, I prefer to chop the kale in a food processor. This makes it much easier for little ones to eat. But if you're cooking just for adults, roughly chopped kale looks a little fancier in the bowl.

- 2 tablespoons extra virgin olive oil
- 1 pound Italian sausage, loose or with casings removed
- 1 large onion, sliced into small wedges
- 4 garlic cloves, minced
- 2 tablespoons dried parsley
- 2 teaspoons dried oregano
- 1 teaspoon dried basil
- 1 teaspoon salt
- 1 teaspoon crushed red pepper flakes (optional)
- 2 (15 ounce) cans tomato sauce
- 4 cups water
- 2 (15 ounce) cans cannellini beans, drained and rinsed
- 2 large bunches kale, center stems removed and leaves torn into bite-sized pieces
- 1 cup grated Parmesan cheese (optional)

1. Prep vegetables and set aside.
2. In a large stockpot, heat oil, then add sausage. Cook until the pink is gone and the sausage crumbles.
3. Add onions to the pot and cook until they are soft and just beginning to turn golden (about 5 minutes). Add garlic and cook for 30 seconds more.
4. Stir in parsley, oregano, basil, 1/2 teaspoon of salt, and 1 teaspoon of crushed red pepper flakes.
5. When the spices are evenly mixed in, add the tomato sauce, water, and beans.
6. Bring to a simmer (about 10 minutes), then add the kale. Cook, covered, until the kale has wilted and the soup is cooked through (about another 5–10 minutes).
7. Check seasonings, adding more salt and crushed red pepper flakes if needed.
8. Before serving, garnish with shredded Parmesan.

CORN CHOWDER

GF, NF	Serves 12	Prep Time: 5 minutes	Cook Time: 25 minutes

This soup is embarrassingly easy to make. It is also embarrassingly easy to have three helpings of—all in one day. Or so I hear from a friend. (Bonus: It's super popular with kids.)

- 1 (32 ounce) bag Southern-style diced hash brown potatoes (or 12 cups diced fresh potatoes)
- 2 pounds pork sausage, loose or with casings removed
- 2 large onions, diced
- 2 (15 ounce) cans sweet corn, drained
- 2 (15 ounce) cans creamed corn
- 6 cups water
- 2 (12 ounce) cans evaporated milk
- 2 1/2 tablespoons Lawry's Seasoned Salt
- 1/4 teaspoon black pepper

1. In a large pot, combine potatoes and water and bring to a boil. Continue boiling until potatoes are tender (about 10 minutes).
2. While the potatoes boil, chop your onion.
3. Next, using a large frying pan, brown sausage until it crumbles and is no longer pink (6–8 minutes). Add onion to sausage and cook until it is lightly golden (5–7 minutes). Drain sausage mixture in a paper towel-lined dish and set aside.
4. To the pot with the potatoes, add sausage and onion mixture, corn, creamed corn, evaporated milk, pepper, and seasoned salt. Simmer until heated through.
5. Check soup to see if it needs more seasoned salt (I usually think it does) or pepper, then keep warm or serve immediately.

AUNT AMY'S VEGETABLE BEEF SOUP

GF, DF, NF	Serves 40 (yes, 40)	Prep Time: 15 minutes	Cook Time: 3.5–4 hours

My Aunt Amy's vegetable beef soup won't feed an army. But it will feed a small battalion. The amount of soup this recipe makes is enormous. So much so that you can feed multiple, very fertile families without even doubling the recipe. I've tried halving it, but the proportions never work out, and then I just have tons of leftover frozen vegetables in my freezer. So if I'm not feeding a small army of other people's children, we eat what we can over the course of four to five days, then freeze the rest. It keeps well for at least six months in the freezer.

You will need a giant pot for this soup. I brown the meat in a heavy-bottomed pan and then cook the actual soup in a 16-quart stock pot. If you don't have an industrial-sized pot, just be prepared to cook the soup in more than one pot.

- 4 pounds beef stew meat
- 8 medium baking potatoes, peeled and diced
- 4 sweet potatoes, peeled and diced
- 4 medium onions, diced
- 48 ounces frozen mixed vegetables (a combination of corn, green beans, carrots, and peas)
- 32 ounces frozen okra
- 2 (28 ounce) cans crushed tomatoes
- 1 (46 ounce) can V8 juice
- 3 cups beef broth
- 3 teaspoons salt
- 2 teaspoons black pepper
- 2 bay leaves
- 3 tablespoons Lowry's Seasoned Salt
- 2/3 cup sugar
- 10 cups water

1. Working in batches, heat oil in heavy-bottomed pan and brown stew meat on all sides.
2. Transfer meat to an extra large stock pot. Add broth, onions, seasoned salt, pepper, and water.
3. Simmer 1 hour.
4. Add all remaining ingredients and continue simmering for at least 2 hours.
5. Check seasonings and keep warm or serve.

POTATO SOUP

V*, NF	Serves 8	Prep Time: 10 minutes	Cook Time: 40 minutes

Over the years, I've tried making various dairy-free potato soups, looking for one that is as good as my favorite potato soup but I can also serve to friends and family who carry the heavy cross of dairy allergies. After a decade plus of searching . . . I've concluded no such soup exists. Sorry! I promise to keep looking. In the meantime, I'm afraid this soup is for dairy lovers only.

- 4 cups baking potatoes, peeled and diced
- 2 onions, diced
- 2 cups (16 ounces) shredded pepper jack or white cheddar cheese
- 4 cups whole milk
- 1/2 cup butter
- 1/2 cup flour
- 1 pound bacon, cooked and crumbled (omit for vegetarian option)
- 8 ounces sour cream
- 1 bunch chives, finely chopped
- salt and pepper to taste

1. Place potatoes and onions in a large pot and just barely cover with water. Bring to a boil. Continue boiling until potatoes are tender (about 10 minutes).
2. Puree half the potatoes and onions in a food processor or blender, slowly adding cooking water until the mixture is smooth but not watery. Drain remaining potatoes in the pot and set aside.
3. In a large pot, melt butter. Add flour and whisk until it forms a roux, cooking for 1–2 minutes until it just begins to turn golden. Slowly add the milk, stirring constantly until mixture begins to thicken.
4. Once thickened, stir in shredded cheese until melted.
5. Add potatoes, onions, and potato puree to milk then liberally add salt and pepper to taste.
6. Serve topped with bacon, sour cream, and chives.

TOMATO BISQUE

GF, V*, NF	Serves 8	Prep Time: 10 minutes	Cook Time: 60 minutes

Everyone needs a good tomato soup recipe for Friday nights in winter. This is ours.

- 4 (28 ounce) cans whole tomatoes, drained
- 8 carrots, peeled and roughly chopped
- 2 onions, quartered
- 2 tablespoons extra virgin olive oil
- 2 tablespoons light brown sugar
- 1 teaspoon salt
- 1/2 teaspoon pepper
- 6 tablespoons salted butter
- 1 teaspoon crushed red pepper flakes
- 4 garlic cloves, minced
- 2 tablespoons tomato paste
- 1/4 cup red wine
- 2 (28 ounce) cans crushed tomatoes
- 3 cups chicken broth (use vegetable broth for vegetarian option)
- 1 cup heavy cream

1. Preheat oven to 400° F and prep vegetables.
2. In a large mixing bowl, combine whole canned tomatoes, carrots, onions, olive oil, and brown sugar; toss until coated.
3. Line an extra large, rimmed baking sheet (or two regular sized baking sheets) with parchment paper and spread vegetables evenly on the pan. Sprinkle with salt and pepper.
4. Roast for 30 minutes or until vegetables start to caramelize, then set aside.
5. Once vegetables are out of the oven, melt butter in a heavy-bottomed stock pot. Add garlic and cook until fragrant (about 1 minute). To the butter and garlic, add the roasted vegetables, crushed tomatoes, tomato paste, wine, and chicken broth and simmer for 15 minutes.
6. Puree bisque using an immersion blender (or puree in batches in a blender, then return to the pot).
7. Add crushed red pepper flakes and cream. After stirring, check seasonings and add more salt and pepper if desired.
8. Keep warm until ready to serve.

CUCUMBER GAZPACHO

GF, DF*, V, VG, NF	Serves 6–8	Prep Time: 10 minutes

In the summer of 2015, my garden produced approximately 546,224 cucumbers. Or maybe it was more like 546. Either way, it was a lot of cucumbers. And I was desperate for new ways to use them. A trip to Savannah, Georgia, and a soup found in a charming little coffee shop not far from Flannery O'Conner's childhood home inspired this particular use.

Gazpacho

- 6 cups (3 pounds) cucumbers, roughly chopped
- 1 1/2 pounds green seedless grapes
- 3 bunches green onions, white parts only
- 6 lemons, juiced
- 1 1/2 cups extra virgin olive oil
- 1 1/2 teaspoons salt
- 1/8 teaspoon pepper

Topping

- 2 pounds tomatoes, quartered
- 1 large cucumber, peeled, seeded, and sliced
- 4 ounces feta cheese (optional)
- 3 lemons, juiced
- 6 tablespoons extra virgin olive oil

1. Put all the ingredients for the gazpacho in a blender and puree until just smooth. Check seasonings and add more salt or pepper if needed, then refrigerate until ready to serve.
2. In a bowl, toss tomatoes, cucumber, lemon juice, and olive oil. Keep at room temperature until ready to serve.
3. Dish gazpacho into individual bowls and top with tomato/cucumber mixture and feta (if using).

CARROT, APPLE & GINGER SOUP

GF*, DF*, V*, VG*, NF	Serves 6–8	Prep Time: 15 minutes	Cook Time: 35 minutes

I've lived in the Pittsburgh region for almost twenty-five years, but I have never adjusted to the endless gray of winters here. On the grayest February days, though, this brilliantly bright soup helps me cope.

I prefer the taste of chicken broth to vegetable broth in this soup. Also, I love the crunch of croutons and the hint of creaminess from the cream. But if you need to make this gluten-free or vegan, the recipe is easily adaptable. Just sub gluten-free bread for regular bread to make the croutons, use vegetable broth instead of chicken broth, and use coconut cream instead of heavy cream (or omit the cream altogether).

- 1 large onion, diced
- 4 tablespoons freshly grated ginger
- 2 garlic cloves, minced
- 2 pounds carrots, peeled and chopped into large pieces
- 3 Granny Smith apples, peeled, cored, and diced
- 6 cups chicken broth (or vegetable broth for vegetarian/vegan option)
- 1 cup heavy cream (or coconut cream), plus more for serving
- 1 1/2–2 teaspoons salt
- pepper
- 3 tablespoons extra virgin olive oil, plus more for drizzling on bread
- 4 slices good bread, cubed

1. Preheat oven to 325° F. Heat 3 tablespoons of oil in a large pot. Add onions and cook until translucent (about 5 minutes). Add the garlic and ginger to the onion and cook another minute more, being careful not to let the garlic burn.
2. Add the apples and carrots, stirring to coat. Cook for 2–3 minutes, then add broth and 1 teaspoon of salt. Bring broth to a boil then reduce heat to medium-low; cook for 20 minutes or until the carrots are tender.
3. While the soup is simmering, spread the cubed bread onto a baking sheet lined with parchment paper, then drizzle generously with olive oil. Bake for 10–15 minutes until bread is toasted but not hard.
4. When the carrots have become fork-tender, puree them using an immersion blender (alternately, working in batches, pour the broth mixture into a food processor or blender and puree until smooth). Add cream and stir. Check the seasoning and, if necessary, add more salt.
5. To serve, ladle soup into individual bowls. Drizzle a little more cream into each bowl, and garnish with croutons and freshly ground pepper.

PUMPKIN TORTELLINI SOUP

NF	Serves 6–8	Prep Time: 5 minutes	Cook Time: 60 minutes

In recent years, my family has spent the day before Thanksgiving driving back to my hometown in Illinois. My parents' failing health (and my dad's eventual death), required us spending most holidays there. But in days gone by, when I hosted Thanksgiving at my home for both friends and family, Wednesday was the day my house started filling up with guests. This pot of soup was always on the menu for that night (and in the fridge the next day for anyone who wanted a light lunch before the big evening meal).

4 tablespoons butter
1 large onion, chopped
8 cups chicken broth
2 (15 ounce) cans pumpkin puree
1/2 cup brown sugar
1/4 teaspoon salt
2 1/2 teaspoons cinnamon
1 1/4 teaspoons ground ginger
1 1/4 teaspoon ground nutmeg
1/2 teaspoon ground cloves
2 cups heavy cream
20 ounces tortellini, fresh or frozen

1. Melt butter over medium-low heat in a heavy-bottomed pan. Add onions and cook until tender (7–10 minutes).
2. Add half the chicken broth and bring to a boil. Reduce heat and simmer, covered, for 15 minutes.
3. Using an immersion blender, puree until smooth (or transfer the broth to a blender, blend until smooth, and then return to the pot).
4. Add the remaining broth, pumpkin puree, brown sugar, salt, and spices. Bring to a boil, then reduce heat and simmer, covered, for at least 10 minutes.
5. To the soup, add the whipping cream and tortellini. Cook for five minutes more or until tortellini are cooked through.
6. Check spices, adding more if desired, and serve.

QUINOA & BLACK BEAN CHILI WITH AVOCADO CREMA

GF, DF, V, VG, NF	Serves 10–12	Prep Time: 15 minutes	Cook Time: 45 minutes

This vegan chili, much beloved by my former roommate Shannon, was once a staple on Friday nights in our old Steubenville house. Now I'm usually too tired to chop much of anything on a Friday night, but it is a fantastic meatless meal just the same.

Chili

- 4 (15 ounce) cans black beans, drained and rinsed
- 2 (6 ounce) cans tomato paste
- 8 cups (64 ounces) vegetable broth
- 2 onions, diced
- 10 garlic cloves, minced
- 2 tablespoons chili powder
- 2 tablespoons cumin
- 2 teaspoons oregano
- 2 teaspoons extra virgin olive oil
- 2 cups peeled sweet potatoes, cut in 2-inch cubes
- 2 cups uncooked quinoa
- 2 teaspoons salt
- 1/2 teaspoon pepper

Avocado Crema

- 6 garlic cloves, minced
- 8 large avocados
- 6 tablespoons freshly squeezed lime juice, plus more to taste
- 6 tablespoons water
- 1 1/2 teaspoons salt

1. In a fine mesh sieve, rinse the quinoa.
2. Heat oil in a large pot over medium heat. Add onions and cook until they are soft and turn golden (about 10 minutes).
3. Add the minced garlic and cook until fragrant (30 seconds–1 minute).
4. Add the tomato paste, spices, salt, and pepper. Cook for about 2 minutes, stirring constantly.
5. Add beans, broth, and potatoes and simmer for 5 minutes, then add the quinoa. Continue cooking for 20–30 minutes, uncovered and stirring frequently, until thickened.
6. While chili cooks, peel and cube avocados. In a food processor, combine avocados with garlic, lime juice, water, and salt. Blend until smooth.
7. If chili is too thick, thin with water. To serve, top with avocado crema.

SORT OF BRIT'S MOM'S CHILI

GF, NF, DF*	Serves 16	Prep Time: 5 minutes	Cook Time: 90 minutes

Brit Fisk is a rancher and one of the loveliest ladies on Instagram I know. A while back, she shared her mom's recipe for chili. Since I had a freezer full of ground beef, I was eager to try it.

Because I am incapable of leaving well enough alone, I did a lot of tweaking to the recipe. The result has become our go-to chili recipe and a favorite for Super Bowl Sundays (when my husband is all about the football and I am all about the snacks). Serve over cornbread or tortilla chips.

- 8 pounds ground beef
- 2 onions, diced
- 1 (16 ounce) can tomato sauce
- 1/2 cup (4 ounces) tomato paste
- 1 1/2 cups water
- 2 (15 ounce) bottles of Guinness Draught Stout
- 4 tablespoons fish sauce
- 2 tablespoons Tabasco sauce
- 2 teaspoons oregano
- 4 teaspoons garlic powder
- 1/2 cup chili powder
- 4 tablespoons brown sugar
- salt and pepper to taste

Toppings

- shredded cheese
- sour cream
- guacamole
- jalapeños

1. Chop onions.
2. Brown ground beef and onion in a large pot. Drain excess grease and return to the pot (you may need to work in batches, depending on the size of your pot).
3. Add remaining ingredients and simmer for one hour.
4. Adjust seasonings to taste and serve with your preferred toppings over cornbread or tortilla chips.

SAUSAGE, SWEET POTATO & KALE SOUP

GF, NF	Serves 10	Prep Time: 15 minutes	Cook Time: 40 minutes

This has been a favorite around here since I concocted it on a cold winter's night, when Toby was a toddler and I was trying to use up extra ingredients in the house before Christmas. It's fast, full of tasty winter vegetables, and, most important, child approved.

- 2 pounds Italian sausage, loose or with casings removed
- 4 large sweet potatoes, peeled and chopped into bite-sized pieces
- 1 (12 ounce) bag kale (or 2 large bunches), center stems removed and chopped (or chopped extra fine in a food processor)
- 2 large onions, peeled and cut into eighths (quartered and then halved)
- 4 garlic cloves, minced
- 10 cups (80 ounces) chicken broth
- 4 tablespoons Italian seasoning
- 2 cups heavy cream
- 1 cup grated Parmesan cheese
- 1–2 teaspoons salt
- 1/4 teaspoon pepper
- 2 tablespoons extra virgin olive oil
- crushed red pepper flakes (optional)

1. In a large, heavy-bottomed pan, heat olive oil over medium high heat. Add onions and a pinch of salt and pepper. Cook until soft (5–6 minutes), then add garlic and cook until fragrant.
2. Add sausage and cook until brown and crumbled. Drain on paper towels.
3. Return sausage and onion to pot and add broth, Italian seasonings, salt, pepper, and sweet potatoes. Cover and bring to a boil. Once boiling, reduce heat to medium and simmer for 7–10 minutes or until potatoes have softened.
4. Add kale and simmer uncovered for 10 minutes more.
5. Add cream and Parmesan. Check seasonings, adding more salt and pepper to taste.
6. To serve, sprinkle each serving with a pinch of crushed red pepper flakes.

PEA SOUP

GF, NF, DF*	Serves: 8	Prep Time: 15 Minutes	Cook Time: 20 Minutes

Twice a year, our family buys half a pig from a local farm. Being on the adventurous side, I don't get overly specific about my cuts and just happily cook whatever they send me. Sometimes, what comes is a lot of ham. From a freezer full of the stuff, this recipe was born (as were several others in the cookbook) as I tried to figure out new and creative ways to serve ham over and over and over again. This soup was one of my greater successes, erasing from my memory the horrid pea soup (made from a dehydrated mix) that my mom used to serve us as kids.

- 1/4 pound bacon
- 1 carrot, peeled and diced
- 1 onion, peeled and diced
- 2 celery stalks, diced
- 3 (12 ounce) bags frozen peas
- 4 cups (32 ounces) chicken broth
- 3 cups (1 1/2 pounds) ham, diced
- 2 teaspoons Montreal steak seasoning, plus more to taste
- 1/2 cup heavy cream, plus more for serving (omit for dairy-free option)
- salt and pepper to taste

1. In a large stockpot, fry bacon until crisp. Remove bacon from pot, leaving 2 tablespoons of grease (drain off any extra).
2. In the remaining bacon grease, sauté diced carrot, onion, and celery until vegetables are soft and onion is translucent (3–5 minutes).
3. Add peas and chicken broth to vegetables and bring to a simmer. Using an immersion blender, puree soup until smooth (if you don't have an immersion blender, transfer to a blender, working in batches, then return to pot).
4. Add ham and steak seasoning to soup and cook until heated through. Add cream and cook a few minutes more. Check for seasoning, adding more salt and pepper as desired.
5. Ladle soup into individual bowls, topping with crumbled bacon and an extra drizzle of cream.

TOMATO, TORTELLINI & SAUSAGE SOUP

NF	Serves: 12	Prep Time: 5 minutes	Cook Time: 25 minutes

This soup is the very definition of cozy. Hot, hearty, and creamy, I make it on repeat all winter long. It also comes together very quickly, making it the perfect dinner on days when time in the kitchen is limited.

- 2 pounds Italian sausage, loose or with casings removed
- 1 large yellow onion, diced
- 12 garlic cloves, minced
- 6 cups (48 ounces) chicken broth
- 4 tablespoons dried parsley
- 4 teaspoons dried oregano
- 2 teaspoons dried basil
- 2 teaspoons salt
- 2 teaspoons crushed red pepper flakes
- 4 (15 ounce) cans tomato sauce
- 4 cups chopped kale, stems removed
- 20 ounces cheese tortellini
- 1 cup heavy cream
- 2 cups grated Parmesan cheese (for serving)

1. In a large stockpot, heat oil, then add in sausage. Cook until the pink is gone and the sausage crumbles.
2. Add onions and cook until soft and just beginning to turn golden (about 5 minutes). Add garlic and cook until fragrant (1 minute).
3. Stir in parsley, oregano, basil, salt, and 1 teaspoon of crushed red pepper flakes.
4. When the spices are evenly mixed in, add the tomato sauce and broth.
5. Bring to a simmer (about 15 minutes), then add the kale, tortellini, and cream.
6. Cook, uncovered until the kale has wilted and the tortellini is tender (about another 5 minutes).
7. Check seasonings, adding more salt and crushed red pepper flakes if desired.
8. Before serving, garnish with grated Parmesan.

HAM & POTATO SOUP

Serves 8	Prep Time: 20 minutes	Cook Time: 40 minutes

This recipe is another to emerge from the "How on earth do I use up all this ham?" winter of 2022–2023. Inspired by a deep freezer full of ham and a delicious soup made by my friend Christina, I came up with this family favorite. We all love it for dinner, but my personal preferred time of day to eat this soup is actually the early morning hours, before anyone else wakes up. Soup for breakfast is absolutely a thing, and if you haven't tried it, start with this one. It will win you over to the cozy side!

1/2 pound bacon
4 cups (2 pounds) ham, diced
1 large red onion, diced
2 celery stalks, chopped
2 carrots, peeled and chopped
3 garlic cloves, minced
4 pounds yellow potatoes, chopped into bite-sized pieces
4 cups (32 ounces) chicken stock
2 cups water
1 cup heavy cream
1/4 cup sherry or white wine
1 tablespoon Lawry's Seasoned Salt
1 bay leaf
1/2 cup grated Parmesan cheese

1. Fry bacon until crisp, then remove from the pan, leaving 3 tablespoons grease behind.
2. In bacon grease, sauté onion, carrot, and celery until onion is translucent (3–5 min). Add garlic and cook 1 minute more.
3. Add potatoes, broth, water, and seasonings and bring to a boil. Cook until potatoes are tender (about 10–15 minutes).
4. Transfer 5 cups of potatoes and broth (making sure the bay leaf doesn't sneak in) to a blender and puree until smooth.
5. Return potato puree to pot and add ham, cream, sherry, and crumbled bacon. Cook until ham and broth are heated through (about 5 minutes). Taste to adjust seasonings.
6. Top with grated Parmesan and serve.

BUTTERNUT SQUASH & SWEET POTATO SOUP

GF, V, NF, DF*	Serves: 8	Prep Time: 10 minutes active, 45 minutes inactive	Cook Time: 20 minutes

As soon as the leaves begin to turn, this soup is on my stove. It is like fall in a bowl. The only thing better than eating it is doing so while an apple crisp bakes in the oven and You've Got Mail *plays on the television.*

- 1 large butternut squash, quartered and seeded
- 4 sweet potatoes, halved
- 2 carrots, chopped
- 2 celery stalks, chopped
- 1 sweet onion, chopped
- 6 cups (48 ounces) chicken broth
- 1 cup heavy cream, plus more for serving (use coconut cream for dairy-free option)
- 1 teaspoon cinnamon
- 1/2 teaspoon nutmeg
- 1/4 teaspoon cloves
- 1 cup (8 ounces) diced pancetta
- 2 tablespoons butter
- extra virgin olive oil
- salt and pepper to taste

1. Preheat oven to 400° F.
2. On a parchment-lined sheet pan, arrange squash and sweet potatoes. Drizzle with olive oil and sprinkle with salt and pepper. Roast for 40–45 minutes until golden and soft. When cool enough to handle, scoop the squash and potato out of their skins and place the flesh in a bowl. Set aside.
3. In an 8-quart stockpot, fry pancetta until it begins to crisp. Then remove it from the pot, leaving fat behind. To the same pan, add butter and melt. Add onions, carrots, and celery and season with salt and pepper. Sauté until soft (about 5 minutes).
4. To the vegetables, add squash, sweet potatoes, chicken broth, and spices, stirring until it comes to a simmer.
5. Using an immersion blender, puree the soup until smooth (alternately, transfer to a blender or food processor).
6. Add cream and heat through, then adjust seasonings as desired.
7. Serve in bowls topped with pancetta and an extra drizzle of cream.

FISH STEW

GF, NF	Serves 8	Prep Time: 10 Minutes	Cook Time: 25 Minutes

This is another Friday favorite. It comes together quickly and is always cozy eating. Whatever you do, though, don't leave out the anchovies. I know they have a bad rap, but I promise, in this dish they are completely necessary. You don't taste them at all, just the umami they lend to the dish. When I accidentally left them out one time, I learned the hard way that they have a huge impact on the stew and its depth of flavor.

I usually add a bit of cream to the kids' bowls, just to tame the spice factor for them.

- 6 cod fillets (if frozen, thawed)
- 2 (14.5 ounce) cans whole peeled tomatoes
- 2 pounds fingerling potatoes, sliced into 1/4-inch rounds
- 6 anchovy fillets
- 1 onion, chopped
- 4 garlic cloves, minced
- 3 tablespoons capers
- 1/2 teaspoon crushed red pepper flakes
- 1/2 cup white wine
- 1 cup grated Parmesan cheese
- extra virgin olive oil
- salt and pepper to taste

1. Fill a medium-sized pot with salted water and bring to a boil.
2. While the water heats, prep the vegetables: slice the potatoes, chop the onion, mince the garlic; then, place the tomatoes and their juices in a bowl and break up the tomatoes into smaller pieces.
3. Pat dry the cod with paper towels, then cut up each fillet into 6–8 pieces. Season with salt and pepper.
4. Once the water is boiling, add the potatoes and cook until tender (10–15 minutes), then drain.
5. In a separate large pot, heat 2 tablespoons of olive oil. Add the onion and a bit of salt and pepper; sauté the onion until soft (2–3 minutes). Add the garlic and cook for about a minute until fragrant. Add the anchovies, capers, and crushed red pepper flakes and cook for about a minute. Add the tomatoes, one cup of water, and a bit more salt and pepper. Cook, stirring occasionally, for about 5 minutes.
6. To the pot with your aromatics, add the cod and potatoes. Cook for five minutes, then add the white wine.
7. Cook for a few minutes more. Add Parmesan, then adjust seasonings to taste before serving.

TABLE LESSONS

Big Flavors, Little People

"Do your kids really eat that?" Anytime I post a picture on social media of a dish I've made for dinner, someone (usually many someones) inevitably asks that.

Sometimes the answer is yes. Sometimes the answer is no. Most of the time, the answer is, "One of them ate all of it, one ate some of it, and one wouldn't touch it." All of which is okay. It doesn't bother me or worry me when the four-year-old won't eat lentils. While I am thrilled when a dinner meets with their resounding approval, their approval is not my goal. If it were, I would just serve them macaroni and cheese every night.

But I don't. And the reason is that I am not cooking to please my three-, four-, and six-year olds' palates. I'm cooking to please my palate and Chris's palate. I'm also cooking for my children's *someday* palates. I'm cooking for the woman and men they will be ten, twenty, or fifty years down the road. I want those selves to have grown up exposed to a world of flavors. I want them to have tasted and tried a thousand different dishes before they leave my house, both because I hope it will help them appreciate the endless variety of deliciousness God has given us through food and because I want them to learn to graciously receive whatever they are served, even if it's not their favorite. I want my children to know they don't have to like something to eat it—that sometimes politeness matters more than pleasure.

I also want them to know that being brave and taking the bite of the food they're sure they will hate can pay off in unexpected ways. Yes, they might discover that they love it, which is always a treat. But they also might discover that they are more capable than they realized of doing hard things. They might find they have more courage, more strength, and more generosity of spirit than they knew they had. And that, in turn, might encourage them to keep being courageous, strong, and generous when they walk away from the table. It might encourage them to do so every day of their life.

So that's why I put steaming plates of risotto in front of my children every week, and that's why I don't worry too much if they don't always appreciate it quite as much as I think they should. Because I am not simply feeding them. I'm also teaching them. I'm trying to help them become gracious and grateful, adventurous and courageous, thoughtful and joyful. I'm helping them become more fully themselves.

The fact that I get to eat lamb biryani and cauliflower galettes in the process is just an added bonus.

RISOTTO

Risottos are, hands down, my favorite dish to cook for company. If there are eight people or fewer around my table, odds are they're eating one of my risottos. Most people do not think of them as an "easy meal" for hosting, but that's just because they're not approaching the cooking of risotto in the right way.

And yes, there is a right way. After cooking risotto approximately 1,246 times for company, this is something I'm willing to stake my claim on and not budge.

So what is the right way?

Here's a hint: It doesn't involve an Instant Pot.

Now that we've gotten that out of the way, let's talk about how you can invest the necessary time in making a risotto when company is on the way.

The Art of Cooking Risotto

Making the perfect risotto for company starts about 90 minutes before people arrive. This is when you want to begin your prep work. Chop your onions, garlic, and any veggies going into the recipe. Get that casing off the Italian sausage. Have your broth ready to go in a small stockpot. Then walk away from the ingredients, clean yourself up (and your house if need be), and start slicing cheese. The cheese is important. It is what will keep your guests and kids occupied while you cook the actual risotto, drink wine, and pretend you're an oh-so-sophisticated Italian chef.

Okay, got that cheese sliced? And crackers, meat, olives, or other snacky foods out? Then, it's time to return to the risotto.

About 15 minutes before guests arrive, bring the broth to a simmer. Not a boil. Not steaming hot. Just a nice low simmer. Now keep it there.

Next, if you need to cook meat, start cooking it now, before people are standing in your kitchen. You can cook the bacon in the oven for convenience. The sausage you'll cook in a large heavy-bottomed pot. After that (or first if there is no meat in the risotto), add your onions, garlic, and eventually any other veggies that need to get cooked into the pot. Yes, cook everything together unless the recipe says otherwise. Onions should be golden and veggies tender when guests arrive.

As soon as the doorbell rings, turn the stove all the way down to the lowest possible simmer and walk away again. Greet you guests. Pour them wine. Send the children off to another room—preferably the most remote room imaginable so the parents can relax—and tell your guests to help themselves to the cheese you've set out in the kitchen. Then get back to cooking.

From this point forward, all you have to do is follow my instructions for cooking risotto. Which basically means (after toasting the rice for a minute) standing at the stove, adding liquid a little bit at a time, stirring until it's absorbed, and drinking wine while you talk to your guests. It will take about 20 to 30 minutes for the rice to get creamy but al dente. And you do not need to worry about guests getting hungry during this time. Because cheese. If the children reappear before dinner is ready, throw some cheese in their general direction too.

Now, a few more risotto tips before I give you specific recipes.

1. Most of the recipes for risotto included here feed six adults. All can be doubled to feed twelve. That is the maximum number of people I recommend cooking risotto for at one time, unless you want to attempt using two big pots for cooking. The pot simply gets too difficult to stir if you try to go beyond twelve servings.

2. Don't worry about what kind of white wine you use. I usually keep a bottle in the fridge, left over from a party. Freshness is not key here. Nor is quality. The cheap stuff works just fine.

3. I always use arborio rice, which, when slowly cooked with broth, will break down and give you that lovely creamy texture. Carnaroli rice is just as good but harder to find. Other rice

(jasmine, basmati, long grain) can be used, but the texture won't be quite right, and you'll miss out on some of the creaminess that is proper to risotto.

4. If you read another recipe for risotto somewhere and it tells you to sauté your onions and the rice in olive oil, ignore that advice. It's wrong. Risotto is always tastiest when the fat you use is butter. I don't know why. Probably science.

5. All the recipes call for chicken broth, but if you want to make the veggie-based ones vegetarian, just swap vegetable broth for the chicken broth.

6. Risotto is a very indecisive dish. It never really knows how much broth it wants until it has it. The ingredients say 8 cups. But depending on the day and the ingredients, I might use slightly more or slightly less. That's why towards the end of the cooking process, you just have to keep tasting. If the rice is crunchy, it needs more liquid. Keep adding more broth, one ladleful at a time, until the crunch is gone. If you start to run out of broth, just add a bit of water to your broth pan.

7. How do you know when to add more broth to the rice? Two ways. First, by sight: if most of the liquid looks like it's been sucked up by the rice, add more. Second, by sound: risotto gets louder and louder the thirstier it gets, especially early in the process. When it starts to hiss and pop, give it a drink.

8. Risotto needs almost constant attention. So when I say stir constantly, I pretty much mean stir constantly. Yes, you can turn away for 30 seconds to wash a pan, sip some wine, or discipline a child, but mostly you need to be standing over the stove, slowly stirring the rice. That being said, the constant stirring is more important at the beginning than at the end, when you can walk away for a minute or two without hurting the dish.

9. Risotto should be served fairly immediately after you finish cooking it. It does not keep well on the stove. So as it's getting close to being done, get whatever else you're serving (bread, brussels sprouts, salad, etc.) out of the oven or refrigerator and onto the table. Summon the masses. Tell the kids to wash their hands. And when you have stirred in the last bit of butter or cheese and checked the rice for appropriate seasoning, whisk that risotto off the stove, onto the table, and into people's bellies.

10. Risotto never tastes as good the next day . . . unless you do this: After the meal is over, lay out a piece of parchment paper, dump the risotto onto it, and shape it into a log. Then wrap it up in the parchment paper, seal it up by wrapping it in another layer of foil, and refrigerate. When ready to eat again, cut it into slices, and fry it in olive oil over medium heat (preferably in a cast iron or non-stick pan). When you do this, it's even better than it was the night before.

Now for the recipes. I'm giving you nine, but as you'll see, once you get the general technique down, there is no end to the different combinations you can put together.

SAUSAGE & MUSHROOM RISOTTO

GF, NF	Serves 6	Prep Time: 20 minutes	Cook Time 50–60 minutes

- 1 pound Italian sausage, loose or with casings removed
- 1 medium sweet onion, diced
- 4 garlic cloves, minced
- 3 cups (8 ounces) white mushrooms, sliced
- 2 red bell peppers, sliced into 1-inch strips
- 2 tablespoons butter
- 8 cups (64 ounces) chicken broth
- 1/2 cup white wine
- 2 cups uncooked arborio rice
- 1 cup grated Parmesan cheese
- salt and pepper to taste

1. In a medium-sized saucepan, bring broth to a simmer (not a boil!).
2. Meanwhile, in a large, heavy-bottomed pot, melt butter over medium-high heat. Add sausage and cook until lightly browned.
3. Add onions to sausage. Lightly add salt and pepper and cook until onions are translucent and lightly golden (4–6 minutes).
4. Add garlic and cook until garlic begins to release its fragrance (30 seconds–1 minute).
5. Add mushrooms, red pepper, and a small amount of salt and pepper to the sausage and onion mix. Cook until veggies have softened and mushrooms have begun releasing liquid (4–6 minutes).
6. Add arborio rice to sausage and veggies. Toss well with other ingredients to coat in fat, and continue to stir for 1–2 minutes, until you hear it start to slightly crackle.
7. Pour in wine, stirring constantly until liquid is absorbed.
8. Continue adding broth, one ladleful at a time, as the liquid absorbs (this will usually be every two minutes). Stir repeatedly throughout this process.
9. When the rice is al dente and creamy in texture, remove from heat and vigorously stir in Parmesan. Add more salt and pepper at this point, if it needs it.
10. Serve immediately.

BACON & SAGE RISOTTO

GF, NF	Serves 6	Prep Time: 25 minutes	Cook Time: 35-40 minutes

1 pound bacon
1 onion, diced
4 garlic cloves, minced
2 tablespoons reserved bacon fat
3 tablespoons butter
2 cups uncooked arborio rice
1/2 cup white wine
8 cups (64 ounces) chicken broth
4 tablespoons roughly chopped fresh sage
2/3 cup grated Parmesan cheese
salt and pepper to taste

1. In a medium-sized stockpot, bring the broth to a simmer (not a boil!).
2. Chop the uncooked bacon into 1–2 pieces. Working in batches if necessary, fry in a large pot until it's well cooked, but not too crispy. Then, drain the bacon onto a paper towel. Pour off the grease, reserving 2 tablespoons for the next step.
3. Heat the reserved bacon grease, plus 1 tablespoon of butter in the same large pot over medium heat. When the butter is melted, add the onions and cook until translucent (about 3–5 minutes).
4. Add garlic and cook for 30–60 seconds more.
5. Add rice. Mix in with the onions and garlic and allow the rice to toast for about 1–2 minutes, stirring frequently so that it doesn't burn.
6. Increase the heat to medium-high. Add wine and stir until absorbed.
7. Begin adding broth slowly, one ladleful at a time. After you've added the first ladle of broth, stir the rice until the liquid is absorbed (about 1–2 minutes). Then, add the next ladleful. Repeat until the rice is creamy and soft but firm to the bite (al dente).
8. Remove from heat. Add in the remaining 2 tablespoons of butter and Parmesan. Stir vigorously until combined.
9. Add sage and bacon. Stir, then taste before adding salt and pepper. (I add just slightly more than 1/4 teaspoon of salt and a few turns of the pepper grinder.)
10. Serve immediately.

ROASTED MUSHROOM RISOTTO

GF, V*, NF	Serves 6	Prep Time: 15 minutes	Cook Time: 40 minutes

9 cups (24 ounces) mixed mushrooms (whatever is available in your local grocery will work: button, shiitake, baby bella, etc.), chopped

1 large onion, diced

8 garlic cloves (6 crushed, 2 minced)

8 sprigs thyme and 1 tablespoon chopped thyme, divided

1 teaspoon crushed red pepper flakes

8 cups (64 ounces) chicken broth (or vegetable broth for vegetarian option)

1/2 cup dry vermouth

4 tablespoons butter

extra virgin olive oil

3 lemons, zested

1 cup grated Parmesan cheese

salt and pepper to taste

1. Preheat oven to 350° F.
2. Spread mushrooms, crushed garlic cloves, and thyme sprigs on a parchment-lined sheet pan; drizzle with olive oil (about 1/4 cup). Sprinkle liberally with salt and pepper. Toss to coat. Roast for 25–30 minutes. Remove from oven and keep warm.
3. Meanwhile, bring broth to a simmer in a stockpot.
4. Melt 2 tablespoons butter in large, heavy-bottomed pan. Add onions, salt and pepper, and sauté over medium high heat until golden (5–7 minutes). Add minced garlic and cook until fragrant (30 seconds–1 minute).
5. Add rice. Toss to coat with butter and onions.
6. Add vermouth. Stir until absorbed.
7. Begin adding broth slowly, one ladleful at a time. After you've added the first ladle of broth, stir the rice until the liquid is absorbed (about 1–2 minutes), then add the next ladleful. Repeat until the rice is creamy and soft, but firm to the bite (al dente).
8. Remove from heat. Add in the remaining 2 tablespoons of butter and Parmesan. Stir vigorously until combined.
9. Add lemon zest, chopped thyme, and check to see if it needs salt or pepper.
10. Transfer to a large serving bowl (or individual plates) and top with roasted mushrooms.
11. Serve immediately.

ROASTED CAULIFLOWER & GRUYÈRE RISOTTO WITH PANCETTA

GF	Serves 6	Prep Time: 15 minutes	Cook Time: 50–60 minutes

- 1 large head cauliflower, chopped into medium- to small-sized florets
- 1 cup (8 ounces) diced pancetta
- 1 small onion, chopped
- 4 tablespoons butter
- extra virgin olive oil
- 4 garlic cloves, minced
- 1/2 cup sherry or dry white wine
- 8 cups (64 ounces) chicken broth
- 1 small bunch sage, half chopped (about 2 tablespoons), half left whole, with leaves removed from stems
- 1/2 cup sliced almonds
- 1 cup grated Gruyère cheese
- 1 1/2 cups grated Parmesan cheese
- salt and pepper to taste

1. Preheat oven to 425° F.
2. Spread cauliflower on a parchment-lined sheet pan. Drizzle liberally with olive oil, salt, pepper, and 1 cup of Parmesan. Roast for 30 minutes, tossing at least once. During the last 5 minutes of cooking, add whole sage leaves and sliced almonds. When done, set aside and keep warm.
3. While cauliflower roasts, bring chicken broth to a simmer.
4. Melt 2 tablespoons of butter in pan. Fry pancetta until it releases its fat and the skin begins to crisp.
5. Add onions, chopped sage, salt, and pepper. Cook until golden (6–9 minutes). Add garlic and cook until fragrant (30 seconds–1 minute).
6. Add rice and toss to coat. Cook for 1–2 minutes until it starts to "pop." Add sherry (or wine). Stir until absorbed.
7. Begin adding broth slowly, one ladleful at a time. After you've added the first ladle of broth, stir the rice until the liquid is absorbed (about 1–2 minutes), then add the next ladleful. Repeat until the rice is creamy and soft but firm to the bite (al dente).
8. Remove from heat; add the remaining 2 tablespoons of butter, Gruyère, and Parmesan. Stir vigorously until combined.
9. Add roasted cauliflower, almonds, sage, and salt and pepper to taste.
10. Serve immediately, garnishing plates or bowls with Parmesan crisps from the cauliflower sheet pan.

CAPRESE RISOTTO

GF, NF	Serves 6	Prep Time: 10 minutes	Cook Time: 45 minutes

8 ounces prosciutto, roughly chopped

1 medium onion, diced

4 garlic cloves, minced

2 cups (16 ounces) cherry or grape tomatoes

8 ounces fresh mozzarella cheese, cubed

1 cup grated Parmesan cheese

1 cup basil, roughly chopped, plus 12 additional leaves, roughly torn, for garnish

2 cups uncooked arborio rice

8 cups (64 ounces) chicken broth

1/2 cup white wine

4 tablespoons butter

2 tablespoons extra virgin olive oil

salt and pepper to taste

1. In a large frying pan, melt 2 tablespoons of butter. Add prosciutto and fry until crisp, set aside and keep warm.
2. Wipe the frying pan clean and add olive oil. When sizzling, add tomatoes. Stir as they begin to heat up and "pop." Roughly smash with a spatula while they continue to cook. Season with salt and pepper. Set aside and keep warm.
3. In a medium-sized stockpot, bring chicken broth to a simmer.
4. In a large, heavy-bottomed pan, melt remaining butter. Add onions and cook until golden (5–7 minutes). Add garlic and tomatoes and cook until fragrant (1 minute). Add in rice, and toss to coat. Toast for 1–2 minutes. Add wine and stir until absorbed.
5. Begin adding broth slowly, one ladleful at a time. After you've added the first ladle of broth, stir the rice until the liquid is absorbed (about 1–2 minutes), then, add the next ladleful. Repeat until the rice is creamy and soft but firm to the bite (al dente).
6. Remove from heat. Add in the mozzarella and Parmesan. Stir vigorously until combined.
7. Add the basil and 2/3 of the crumbled prosciutto. Stir until combined. Check for seasoning, adding more salt and pepper to taste.
8. Immediately before serving, top the risotto (either in the pot or individual bowls) with torn basil and crispy prosciutto.

SPRING VEGETABLE RISOTTO

GF, V, NF	Serves 6	Prep Time: 10 minutes	Cook Time: 60 minutes

1 bunch asparagus, trimmed and cut into 2-inch pieces

2 cups shelled sugar snap peas

1 bunch green onions, sliced, with white and green parts separated

4 garlic cloves, minced

2 cups uncooked arborio rice

8 cups (64 ounces) chicken broth

1/2 cup white wine

6 tablespoons butter

2/3 cup grated Parmesan cheese

2/3 cup mascarpone cheese

12–15 mint leaves, chopped

salt and pepper to taste

1. Bring a large pot of salted water to boil. While it boils, fill a large bowl with ice water and set aside. Once the water in the pot is boiling, add asparagus. Allow to boil for 2–4 minutes (depending on thickness) until just tender. Remove from pot with tongs and place immediately in ice water to stop the cooking process. After 1 minute, drain and set aside.
2. Repeat the process with the peas: bring a large pot of water to boil. Prepare an ice water bath. Add peas and boil for 1–2 minutes, until bright green. Drain peas, then immediately transfer to ice water bath. After 1 minute, drain and set aside.
3. In a medium stockpot, bring chicken broth to a simmer.
4. In a large heavy-bottomed pot, melt 2 tablespoons of butter. Add white bottoms of scallions and garlic and a dash of salt and pepper. Cook for 1–2 minutes or until garlic begins to turn golden. Add rice and toast for 1–2 minutes. Add wine and stir until all the liquid is absorbed.
5. Begin adding broth slowly, one ladleful at a time. After you've added the first ladle of broth, stir the rice until the liquid is absorbed (about 1–2 minutes), then, add the next ladleful. Repeat until the rice is creamy and soft but firm to the bite (al dente).
6. Remove from heat. Add in the mascarpone, Parmesan, and remaining butter. Stir vigorously until combined. Add vegetables and stir again. Check seasonings and add salt and pepper to taste.
7. Serve immediately, adding the mint either to the top of the serving dish or individual servings.

BUTTERNUT SQUASH RISOTTO

GF	Serves 6	Prep Time: 25 minutes	Cook Time: 45 minutes

1 medium butternut squash, peeled and cut into 1-inch cubes

2 tablespoons extra virgin olive oil

1 pound sweet Italian sausage, loose or with casings removed

1 medium onion, diced

4 garlic cloves (2 cloves smashed, 2 cloves minced)

3 tablespoons butter

2 cups uncooked arborio rice

1/2 cup sherry

8 cups chicken broth

1/2 cup grated Parmesan cheese

1/4 cup pine nuts

1/4 cup balsamic glaze, store-bought or homemade (see below)

salt and pepper to taste

Balsamic Glaze

1 cup balsamic vinegar

1/2 cup brown sugar

1. Preheat oven to 400° F.
2. If making the Balsamic Glaze, do this first: in a small pot, combine vinegar and sugar. Bring to a simmer and allow it to continue cooking, stirring frequently, until it is reduced by about half (usually 10 minutes). Remove from heat and allow it to cool slightly. Then transfer to a mason jar.
3. Next, in a large frying pan, over low heat, lightly toast pine nuts. Set aside.
4. In a large bowl, toss the butternut squash with garlic, olive oil, 2 teaspoons of salt, and a couple turns of fresh cracked pepper. Spread the squash out on a rimmed, parchment-lined baking sheet and cook at 400° F for 20–25 minutes or until the bottoms are golden and the squash is tender. Once done, set aside and cover with foil to keep warm.
5. In a medium-sized stock pot, bring the broth to a simmer (not a boil).
6. Once the broth is simmering, melt 2 tablespoons of butter in a large, heavy-bottomed pot over medium heat. Add the sausage and cook until almost all the pink is gone.

(continued on next page ⇨)

7. Add the onion and continue cooking until the sausage is crumbled and the onion is translucent. Add garlic and cook for 30–60 seconds more.
8. When the garlic begins to release its fragrance, stir the rice into the pot. Allow the rice to toast for about 1–2 minutes, stirring frequently so that it doesn't burn.
9. Increase the heat to medium-high. Add sherry; stir until absorbed.
10. Begin adding broth slowly, one ladleful at a time. After you've added the first ladle of broth, stir the rice until the liquid is absorbed (about 1–2 minutes), then add the next ladleful. Repeat until the rice is creamy and soft but firm to the bite (al dente).
11. Remove from heat and fold in the Parmesan, remaining butter, and salt to taste. Stir vigorously.
12. Next, fold in the butternut squash and pine nuts.
13. When plating the risotto, drizzle each serving with the balsamic glaze. Serve immediately.

The Euphoria

My friend Janet's signature drink has become a winter favorite of ours, as well. Whatever you do, though, don't skip the sage. It's what makes it a cozy Thanksgiving and Christmas favorite that pairs so well with cranberries and cinnamon and other savory spiced dishes.

2 ounces gin

1/2 ounce St. Germaine (or elderflower liqueur)

1/2 ounce lemon juice, freshly squeezed

2 fresh sage leaves

1. In a cocktail shaker, gently muddle one sage leaf and lemon juice.
2. Fill the shaker with ice and add gin and St. Germaine. Shake while saying one Hail Mary.
3. Pour into an ice-cold glass and garnish

SAUSAGE & CARROT RISOTTO WITH PESTO

GF	Serves 6	Prep Time: 15 minutes	Cook Time: 25–30 minutes

1 pound Italian sausage, loose or with casings removed

1 large red onion, diced

2 garlic cloves, minced

3 large carrots, peeled and shredded

1/4 cup pesto

1/2 cup grated Parmesan cheese

2 tablespoons butter

2 cups uncooked arborio rice

1/2 cup sherry

8 cups chicken broth

salt and pepper to taste

1. Prep all your ingredients: Chop the onion, mince the garlic, shred the carrots (best done using a box grater), shred the cheese.
2. In a medium-sized stock pot, bring the broth to a simmer (not a boil!).
3. In a deep-sided pan or large pot, melt butter, then add sausage. Cook until browned. Add the onion and a pinch of salt and pepper. Sauté over medium heat for 5 minutes until it softens and becomes translucent.
4. Add carrots with another pinch of salt and pepper and cook for a few minutes more.
5. Add garlic and cook for 30–60 seconds more.
6. Add rice. Toast for about 1–2 minutes, stirring frequently so that it doesn't burn.
7. Increase the heat to medium-high. Add sherry and stir until absorbed.
8. Begin adding broth slowly, one ladleful at a time and stirring constantly. After you've added the first ladle of broth, stir the rice until the liquid is absorbed (about 1–2 minutes) then, add the next ladleful. Repeat until the rice is creamy and soft, but firm to the bite (al dente).
9. Remove from heat. Stir in the Parmesan and pesto, until combined. Add more salt and pepper to taste.

RISOTTO WITH SCALLOPS & BROWN BUTTER

GF, NF	Serves 6	Prep Time: 5 minutes	Cook Time: 30 Minutes

3 cups uncooked arborio rice

1 medium sweet onion, diced

2 garlic cloves, minced

1 1/3 cup grated Parmesan cheese

1/2 cup salted butter

1/2 cup white wine

12 cups (96 ounces) seafood stock

1 pound sea scallops

1 1/2 cups fresh greens (such as arugula and kale), chopped into thin ribbons

extra virgin olive oil

salt and pepper to taste

Note: If you cannot find seafood stock and don't have the time to make it, a good substitute is half chicken broth and half water.

1. In a medium-sized stock pot, bring the broth and water to a simmer (not a boil!).
2. Melt 2 tablespoons of butter in a large pot or deep-sided pan over medium heat. When the butter is melted, add the onions and cook until translucent (about 3–5 minutes).
3. Add garlic and cook for 30–60 seconds more.
4. Add rice. Mix in with the onions and garlic and allow the rice to toast for about 1–2 minutes, stirring frequently so that it doesn't burn.
5. Increase the heat to medium-high. Add wine, stirring until absorbed.
6. Begin adding broth slowly, one ladleful at a time. After you've added the first ladle of broth, stir the rice until the liquid is absorbed (about 1–2 minutes), then add the next ladleful. Repeat until the rice is creamy and soft, but firm to the bite (al dente).
7. Take a short break from stirring the risotto to take the scallops out of the fridge, pat them dry with a paper towel, and sprinkle with salt.

(continued on next page ⇨)

8. When the risotto is almost done, heat 2 tablespoons of olive oil in a large frying pan. When the oil is hot enough that a drop of water sizzles when dropped in the pan, add scallops in a single layer, not touching. Cook 3 minutes without moving. Flip and cook another 3 minutes. Remove to plate and cover with foil to keep warm.
9. When the risotto is finished, remove from heat. Add Parmesan and stir vigorously until combined. Add greens and stir gently until combined. Add salt and pepper to taste.
10. In a small sauce pan, melt remaining butter and continue to cook, stirring almost constantly, until the solids have turned a deep, dark, golden brown and the foam has mostly settled (about 3–5 minutes).
11. Divide risotto into bowls. Evenly divide scallops and place on top of rice. Drizzle browned butter over bowls and serve.

Aviation Advent Cocktail

While the classic Aviation includes maraschino liquor, we prefer ours a little lighter and sub in cherry simple syrup instead. You can make you own simple syrup and add cherry juice to it or simply use the liquid from a jar of maraschino cherries. And while technically you can drink this cocktail year-round, the lovely lavender color make it extra fun to drink during Advent (or Lent if you're not giving up alcohol for forty days).

2 ounces gin
1/2 ounce lemon juice, freshly squeezed
1/2 ounce cherry simple syrup
1/4 ounce Crème de Violette
maraschino cherry

1. Fill a shaker halfway with ice.
2. Add lemon juice, cherry syrup, Crème de Violette, and gin.
3. Shake vigorously while saying one Hail Mary and pour into an ice cold Martini

PRACTICAL HOSPITALITY

The Magical Art of Hosting with Little Ones

When Chris and I first brought Toby home, some people thought my days of cooking and hosting would come to a screeching halt. But those people were wrong. The hosting continued. It just continued differently.

During those first few crazy years, when babies were coming fast and furious and we had three children aged two and under, I stopped hosting on weeknights. It was just too much to get up early to write, care for three little ones all day, keep the house tidy, and get a meal on the table for guests by 5:30 p.m. So, for a season, we kept dinner parties to the weekends, when Chris was around and could keep the babies occupied while I tidied and cooked. Now that I have one child approaching the age of reason and two more in preschool, I can handle weeknight guests again—not large dinner parties; those still happen on Saturdays or Sundays, but dear friends who don't mind the mess or the crazy are always welcome.

The second thing that changed when babies came was the menu. In my single days, I experimented, innovated, and got all kinds of creative in the kitchen (hence the recipes in this book). I still like to get creative in the kitchen, but not when guests are coming. My brain can only multitask so much, so I now serve guests simple recipes that I know well and can't ruin, no matter how many toddler-induced distractions arise while I cook. Recipes that I can prep ahead and keep warm are also current favorites.

> ***My brain can only multitask so much, so guests are now served simple recipes that I know well and can't ruin, no matter how many toddler-induced distractions arise while I cook.***

The third thing that helps is not a change I made. It's actually a change I didn't make. When the babies came, I didn't stop inviting friends without babies. I kept on inviting my wonderful

single friends and empty nester friends. These are the people who are too often left out of our "couples only" culture of socializing. They also are generally more than happy to hold a baby or entertain a small child while I cook. Making sure to include them as much as possible is a gift to them and me.

> *Our home is often chaotic, crazy, and loud. But it's also beautiful, joyful, and full of life.*

What else has helped me keep opening my home to others, even with little ones perpetually underfoot?

Two things that I have mentioned elsewhere: I don't do special kids' meals for my friends' children, and I don't get hung up on housekeeping perfection. Crackers and shut doors work wonders.

Paper plates also can come in handy. I'm not sure if, during all those glorious parties of my childhood, I ever ate off a single real plate. Paper plates were all the adults ever gave us. What mattered were the relationships, not how elegant the china and flatware were, and that's what I still remind myself when I start to feel the pressure to make my table look Pinterest perfect.

Last of all, I don't try to do it all by myself. When someone asks, "What can I bring?" I tell them. Or, more accurately, I give them choices. I say: "Either a dessert or salad would be helpful." Or "Wine or bread would be nice. What works for you?" I also don't turn down offers of help with dishes or clearing the table. Part of hosting is giving to people: it's loving them through service. But part of hosting is also receiving: it's letting people love you back by allowing them to help you when you genuinely need help.

And that's how I do it. There's nothing really magical about it. Unless you consider detachment from perfectionism magic. Our home is often chaotic, crazy, and loud. But it's also beautiful, joyful, and full of life. It's good to invite people into that chaos and into the joy. They go together in this season. I could pretend otherwise, but that would involve never inviting anyone into our home for the indefinite future. And that would be a far greater loss than the occasional loss of my pride that occurs when something goes awry with a dinner party.

ENTRÉES

Back when I hosted my glorious Thursday Night Dinners, I never had to worry about salad or dessert or wine; my friends took care of those. That left me free to experiment and concoct and create a whole roster of recipes that could feed a large family . . . or many large families. Marriages and moves and changing seasons of life eventually brought those Thursday Night Dinners to an end. But the recipes to which they gave rise live on, and, more importantly, so do the friendships that grew with every shared meal. These meals helped make strangers my friends and friends my family. My prayer is that they do the same in your home.

LAMB & SWEET POTATO STEW

GF, DF, NF	Serves 8	Prep Time: 15 minutes	Cook Time: 2 hours, 10 minutes

This is the first recipe I shared on my old blog, The Catholic Table. *My dad invented a version of it years ago as an excuse to eat lamb when my mom (who hates lamb) was out of town. With a little bit of tinkering, I've since converted many a non-lamb lover with this stew. (Never my mom, though.)*

- 3 pounds bone-in lamb shoulder
- 1/4 cup sweet vermouth
- 4 (15 ounce) cans stewed tomatoes
- 2 cups (16 ounces) white button mushrooms
- 4 tablespoons sugar
- 4 large sweet potatoes, peeled and chopped
- 5–6 tablespoons extra virgin olive oil
- 1 tablespoon Cajun seasoning (I use Tony Chachere's)
- 4 garlic cloves, peeled and lightly crushed
- fresh rosemary (optional)
- 2 teaspoons salt
- pepper

1. Season meat with a sprinkling of salt and pepper.
2. In a large pot, heat 2 tablespoons olive oil over medium-high heat. Once it's hot enough to sizzle (go ahead and test with a few drops of water), add the whole pieces of lamb shoulder. Brown on both sides (about 2–3 minutes per side). You will likely need to do this in batches.
3. With all the meat back in the pot, add vermouth, scraping up any browned bits on the bottom of the pan.
4. Stir in the tomatoes, sliced mushrooms, sugar, and 2 teaspoons of salt.
5. Reduce heat to low. Cover and simmer for 2 hours.
6. When the stew is about 45 minutes from being done, preheat oven to 400° F. Line a rimmed baking sheet with parchment paper. Spread out the sweet potatoes and crushed garlic. Drizzle with remaining oil and season with Cajun spice. Roast for 25 minutes or until the potatoes are tender and lightly browned.
7. After the meat has simmered for at least 2 hours, remove the lamb from the pot and separate the meat from the bone. Cut the meat into bite-sized pieces, then return to the pot, discarding the bones.
8. Add roasted sweet potatoes and check seasoning to taste, adding more salt, sugar, or Cajun seasoning if desired. Keep warm on the stove until ready to serve. Before serving, garnish with a sprig or scattering of fresh rosemary.

SAUSAGE & PESTO PASTA

Serves 6	Prep Time: 5 minutes	Cook Time: 20 minutes

Toby calls this dish "Mommy's best pasta." I'm not sure if this is accurate, but you can decide for yourself.

- 1 pound Italian sausage, loose or with casings removed
- 1 pound cavatappi pasta
- 2 cups cherry tomatoes
- 1 lemon
- 8 ounces pesto
- 1 cup ricotta cheese
- 4 tablespoons mascarpone cheese
- 1/2 cup grated Parmesan cheese
- 1 cup basil leaves, stems removed
- 1/2 tablespoon crushed red pepper flakes
- 2 garlic cloves, minced
- extra virgin olive oil
- salt and pepper to taste

1. Bring a large pot of salted water to boil. Once boiling, add pasta and cook until al dente. Drain and return to pot and cover to keep warm.
2. Meanwhile, prepare vegetables: peel and mince garlic, zest lemon, juice lemon, halve tomatoes.
3. Make lemon ricotta: Combine ricotta cheese with lemon zest and juice. Season with salt and pepper to taste.
4. In a large pan, heat a small amount of olive oil. Add sausage and brown. When sausage is cooked through, add garlic and cook for 1 minute more.
5. To the pan of sausage, add pasta, mascarpone, and pesto. Toss until combined, then add tomatoes. Cook for 2–3 minutes more, until tomatoes have started to release their juice. At the last minute, add fresh basil leaves.
6. Serve immediately with a sprinkling of Parmesan and a spoonful of lemon ricotta on top.

BEER & BOURBON SHEPHERD'S PIE

GF, NF	Serves 8	Prep Time: 90 minutes	Cook Time: 35 minutes

This is not a simple recipe. I'm sorry. This will make a total mess of your kitchen, and there are many steps. None of them are complicated, though, and the results are worth it. Plus, if you time it right, you can clean up the mess while this bakes so none of your guests will be any the wiser.

1 small head garlic, plus 7 more cloves (5 smashed, 2 minced)

2 1/2 pounds russet potatoes, peeled and chopped

1/4 cup heavy cream

1/2 cup whole milk (plus a little more if needed)

4 tablespoons butter

2 egg yolks

2 cups butternut squash, peeled and chopped

1 medium turnip, peeled and chopped

1 medium yellow onion, chopped

1 pound ground lamb

1/2 pound ground veal

2 1/2 tablespoons cornstarch

1 cup chicken broth

3 teaspoons tomato paste

2 teaspoons Worcestershire sauce

1 bottle stout (such as Guinness)

1 1/2 tablespoons brown sugar

2 tablespoons fresh rosemary, roughly chopped

a healthy splash of bourbon, which I think translates to 3–4 tablespoons

2 teaspoons fresh thyme, roughly chopped

4 ounces Gruyère cheese, shredded

salt and pepper to taste

1. Preheat oven to 400° F. Peel the outer layer of skin from one head of garlic, trim the top off, and drizzle with olive oil. Wrap in foil and roast for 40 minutes. Remove and let cool.
2. While the garlic roasts, prepare your potatoes. Put potatoes in a large pot, cover with cool water, and bring to a boil. When the potatoes are fork tender, drain the water and mash them. Then, using a hand-mixer or stand mixer, whip in the butter, cream, milk, a dash of pepper, and 1 teaspoon salt. Squeeze the roasted garlic out of the skin and into the potatoes. Add more milk if the potatoes seem too dry and more salt if they seem too bland. Lastly, add your egg yolks and mix until combined. Keep warm in a crockpot until ready to use.

3. Once the potatoes are finished, arrange squash, turnip, and smashed garlic on a baking sheet lined with parchment paper, drizzle with 2–3 tablespoons of olive oil, and sprinkle with 3 pinches of salt, plus a couple turns of the pepper mill.
4. Roast squash, turnip, and smashed garlic at 400° F for 25 minutes. When done, remove from oven and set aside.
5. Turn oven down to 375°.
6. While the vegetables roast, add 2 tablespoons of olive oil to a large pot. When the oil begins to glisten, add onions, ground meat, and 1 teaspoon of salt, plus a dash of pepper. Brown well, then drain off most (but not all) of the fat.
7. Return meat and onion mixture to pan and add chopped garlic. Cook for a minute or until garlic gives off its aroma. Add in corn starch and stir until you can no longer see it. Then, add broth, tomato paste, Worcestershire sauce, beer, and brown sugar. Bring to a boil, then reduce heat, cover, and let simmer for 10–15 minutes until the sauce is reduced and thickened, stirring occasionally.
8. When the sauce has thickened, add the roasted vegetables, thyme, and 1 tablespoon of rosemary to the meat mixture. Taste for seasonings and add more salt and brown sugar if necessary. Lastly, add your "healthy" splash of bourbon.
9. Pour meat mixture into a large deep-sided baking dish (9 x 13-inch or something similar). Add your potato layer, starting on the outside and working in. Spread smooth with a spatula, making sure the sides are sealed shut (this is very important; if you start just any old place or leave breathing room along the edges, the mixture will bubble up, and you won't have that pretty top layer).
10. Bake the pie in the oven on top of a foil-lined baking sheet at 375° for 35 minutes.
11. Five minutes before the pie is done, sprinkle with shredded Gruyère.
12. When the pie is done, remove from oven and let cool for 10 minutes.
13. Sprinkle the pie with the remaining fresh rosemary immediately before serving.

LAMB BIRYANI

GF, DF, V*, NF	Serves 8	Prep Time: 30 minutes Inactive, 30 minutes Active	Cook Time: 35 minutes

One of my biggest complaints about Steubenville has always been the total absence of Indian restaurants. So, long ago, I learned to cook my own Indian food. This lamb and rice dish is my greatest success.

Many of the spices can't be found in your local grocery story, but any Indian grocery store will have them. You also can order most through Amazon or other online grocers.

To make this recipe vegetarian, swap out the lamb for 2 pounds of sautéed button mushrooms. Everything else stays the same. It's almost as good that way. Almost.

Rice

- 2 cups basmati rice
- 10 cups water
- 6 black peppercorns
- 4 whole cloves
- 4 green cardamom pods
- 1 half-inch cinnamon stick
- 2 bay leaves

Lamb Mixture

- 1/4 cup ghee
- 1 pound ground lamb
- 1 (15 ounce) can chickpeas, drained
- 6 whole black peppercorns
- 6 green cardamom pods
- 2 whole cloves
- 1 teaspoon cumin seeds
- 36 curry leaves, roughly torn
- 2 tablespoons dried mustard
- 3 jalapeño peppers, seeded and diced
- 1 teaspoon ground turmeric
- 1 teaspoon ground coriander
- 2 teaspoons salt
- 1 teaspoon curry powder
- 1 (15 ounce) can coconut milk
- 1/4 teaspoon cracked peppercorns
- 3/4 cup cilantro, chopped

Yogurt Sauce

- 1 cup whole milk yogurt (regular or Greek)
- 4 garlic cloves, minced
- 2 tablespoons extra virgin olive oil
- 2–4 tablespoons water
- salt and pepper to taste

1. Thirty minutes before you're ready to start cooking, put the rice in a bowl, cover with water, and soak for 30 minutes. Pour into a colander, then rinse and drain.
2. Preheat the oven to 350° F.

(continued on next page ⇨)

3. Combine the water and spices for the rice in a large pot. Bring to a boil. Add rice and stir. Once it returns to a boil, reduce heat to simmer and cover. Cook for 6 minutes, then drain and set aside.
4. In a large skillet, over medium-high heat, cook the ghee, peppercorns, cardamom pods, cloves, and cumin seeds until the cumin starts to brown (about 2 minutes).
5. Add the curry leaves, dried mustard, diced peppers, turmeric, and salt, stirring often. Cook for 1 minute.
6. Reduce the heat to low. Add the coriander and cook for another minute, continuing to stir.
7. Increase the heat to medium-high and add the ground lamb. Cook until the meat is browned and there is no visible pink.
8. Mix in the curry powder and chickpeas. Then stir in the coconut milk. Bring to a vigorous simmer and cook until the liquid is reduced by half (about 10–12 minutes). Stir in 1/4 teaspoon of black pepper, check to see it the dish needs more salt, and remove from heat.
9. In a covered casserole dish greased with butter, layer 1/3 of the rice, 1/2 of the lamb mixture, and 1/3 of the cilantro. Repeat and top with the remaining third of the rice. Cover dish tightly with foil and a lid.
10. If making this ahead of time, you can refrigerate it at this point for up to 4 hours, then bake once guests arrive.
11. Bake in the oven for 35 minutes.
12. While the biryani cooks, make the yogurt sauce. In a small bowl, whisk together yogurt, garlic, and olive oil. Slowly add in water, 1 tablespoon at a time, until reaching the desired consistency. It should be thin but not watery. Season with salt and pepper to taste.
13. When the biryani is cooked through, remove from oven and toss before serving. Garnish with remaining cilantro and serve with the yogurt sauce on the side.

BACON-JALAPEÑO MACARONI & CHEESE

NF	Serves 12	Prep Time: 45 minutes	Cook Time: 30 minutes

For my fortieth birthday, my friends threw me the loveliest wine and cheese tasting party. We all ate our weight in cheese that night, but somehow, there were pounds and pounds left over. In the weeks that followed, I got creative about how to use up that cheese. This concoction, however, was my masterpiece.

It's not an exact science, as at the time I was just trying to use up expensive cheese. In the years since, I've replicated it pretty closely by sticking with the same general portions of hard and soft cheeses. So feel free to experiment with what cheeses you use, just sticking with the same basic ratio.

- 1 pound thick-cut bacon
- 1 pound tofette or orecchiette pasta
- 9 tablespoons butter
- 1 small red onion, minced
- 4 garlic cloves, minced
- 1/2 cup flour
- 1 tablespoon dry mustard
- 2 cups whole milk
- 2 cups heavy cream
- 2 teaspoons paprika
- 2 cups shredded hard cheeses (a mix of Manchego, Romano, Asiago, etc.)
- 4 cups shredded soft cheeses (a mix of Beemster goat, Gouda, white cheddar, Gruyère, etc.), divided
- 1 teaspoon salt, plus more for pasta water
- freshly ground black pepper
- 1/3 cup sliced pickled jalapeños, plus 1–2 teaspoons, diced
- 2 cups panko bread crumbs
- crushed red pepper flakes (optional)

1. Preheat oven to 375° F.
2. Lay out bacon on a parchment-lined baking sheet. Cook for 20–30 minutes (depending on thickness of bacon) or until the bacon is cooked but not crispy. Drain and set aside. Reduce the oven temperature to 350° F.
3. While the bacon cooks, bring a large pot of salted water to a rolling boil. Add pasta and cook until al dente, about 10 minutes. Drain, return to the pot, and cover to keep warm.
4. When the bacon has cooled, chop into bite-sized pieces and set aside.

(*continued on next page* ⇨)

5. In another large, heavy-bottomed pot, melt 6 tablespoons of butter. Add onion and cook for 5 minutes or until just soft. During the last minute of cooking, add the garlic. When the garlic begins to release its fragrance, add in the mustard and flour to form a roux. Whisk to combine, and keep stirring and moving the roux for 2 to 3 minutes.
6. Add the milk, cream, and paprika. Whisk until all lumps disappear. Continue whisking at a simmer for 10 minutes.
7. Gradually, stir in all the hard cheeses, and half the soft cheeses, plus salt and pepper, until the cheese has melted. Remove from heat and stir in the bacon and jalapeño slices. Then fold in the pasta.
8. Pour half the pasta and cheese mixture into a, large, deep, greased baking dish (mine measures 12 x 8.5 x 3-inch). Top with remaining soft cheeses, then pour remaining pasta and cheese sauce into the dish. Set aside.
9. In a frying pan, melt 2 tablespoons of butter. Stir in bread crumbs until coated.
10. Scatter the breadcrumbs on top of the pasta and cheese and top with 1–2 teaspoons of chopped pickled jalapeños.
11. Bake for 25–30 minutes at 350° F or until the top is golden brown.
12. Serve hot, with a sprinkling of crushed red pepper flakes.

SIMPLE INDIAN DHAL

GF, DF*, V, VG*, NF	Serves 8	Prep Time: 15 minutes	Cook Time: 30–40 minutes

Dhal is Indian peasant food at its best. This version is a traditional recipe from a friend, modified by me based on what spices I could find at Kroger. Back when I was single, I would mix up a double batch of this on Monday and eat it for lunch all week long. It is some of my favorite comfort food, and just writing about it makes me want to go whip up a batch right now.

Dhal

- 3 tablespoons ghee (or coconut oil for dairy-free, vegan option)
- 2 teaspoons cumin seeds
- 6 whole cloves
- 8 green cardamom pods
- 2 cups red or green lentils, picked over, washed, and drained
- 1 teaspoon ground turmeric
- 1/4 teaspoon ground cinnamon
- 8 cups water
- 3 teaspoons salt (or to taste)

Tempering Oil

- 2 tablespoons ghee (or coconut oil for dairy-free, vegan option)
- 1 large sweet onion, finely diced
- 6 garlic cloves, minced
- 4 inches fresh ginger, peeled and minced
- 2 jalapeño peppers, seeded and minced

For Serving

- 4 cups jasmine or basmati rice, cooked
- 1/4–1/2 teaspoon cayenne pepper (optional)
- 1/2 cup fresh cilantro, chopped
- 1 cup Greek yogurt
- 1 garlic clove, minced
- 1 tablespoon extra virgin olive oil

13. While the rice cooks, heat 3 tablespoons of ghee in a large saucepan with a lid.
14. Add the cumin, cloves, and cardamom. Cook, stirring, until the cumin turns a golden brown color (about 1 minute).
15. Add the lentils, turmeric, water, cinnamon, and salt. Bring to a boil and skim froth well. Turn down the heat and simmer, covered, until the lentils are soft and easily broken up by a whisk (15 to 30 minutes depending on which lentils you use. Red take less time; green take more). If the lentils break up when whisked, continue whisking, until they resemble a chunky puree.

(continued on next page ⇨)

16. While the lentils are cooking, make your cooling sauce. Mix together garlic, yogurt, and olive oil. Slowly add water 1 tablespoon at a time, until the sauce has reached your desired consistency. Season with salt and pepper to taste.
17. As the lentils continue to cook, prepare the tempering oil. Mince the garlic, jalapeno, ginger, and cilantro. Heat the remaining ghee in a small frying pan over medium-high heat. Add the onion and cook until golden and slightly brown (4 to 5 minutes).
18. Add the garlic, ginger, and jalapenos. Cook just enough to mellow the flavor of all three—about 30 seconds.
19. Before serving, stir half of the tempering oil into the dhal along with half the cilantro. Simmer for 5 minutes. Keep warm on the stove until ready to eat.
20. Serve over rice and top with remaining tempering oil, cilantro, cooling sauce, and cayenne pepper (if using).

Paloma

They say necessity is the mother of invention. This cocktail concurs. It's not a traditional Paloma. It is the Paloma I was able to make on a fine spring day when I had a hankering for this lighter, fresher version of a Margherita but did not have all the necessary ingredients. In the end, though, I loved what I cobbled together even more than the Palomas I'd previously tasted. So this is now our standard recipe.

- 1 1/2 ounces freshly squeezed grapefruit juice
- 1/2 ounce freshly squeezed lemon juice
- 1 ounce simple syrup
- 1 1/2 ounce tequila
- 1–2 ounces lime-flavored sparkling water

In a tall glass, mix together the juices, simple syrup, and tequila. Add ice. Top with sparkling water, adding more or less depending on your preference.

CHRISTMAS EVE BEEF TENDERLOIN

GF, NF	Serves 8	Prep Time: 70 minutes (10 active)	Cook Time: 40 minutes

When I was growing up, my family never did complicated Christmas dinners. Instead, we had appetizers, drinks, and the world's best beef tenderloin sliders. My dad started making the beef tenderloin almost twenty years ago after my grandma passed away and our family inherited Christmas hosting duties. He made it every year until the last few years before his death, when the cooking duties passed to my sisters and me. Now, even on the Christmases when we can't make it back to Illinois, this beef tenderloin is still on the menu. Cut it thick and serve with horseradish (or horseradish sauce) and mashed potatoes. Or slice it thin and serve it on silver dollar buns (also with horseradish).

6 pounds beef tenderloin, trimmed (I usually buy two smaller tenderloins as they cook more evenly this way)

1 cup butter, softened

2 bunches Italian parsley, roughly chopped

1 cup Dijon mustard

4 teaspoons salt

1 cup black peppercorns, freshly ground in a coffee grinder

2 cups mayonnaise (Duke's Real Mayonnaise tastes best; Sir Kensington's Avocado Oil Mayonnaise is the best-tasting seed-oil-free option)

horseradish

1. About 60 minutes before cooking, remove meat from refrigerator and bring to room temperature.
2. Preheat oven to 450° F.
3. Mix together butter, mustard, parsley, pepper, salt, and Dijon mustard. Slather over the tenderloins, coating on 3 sides (don't worry about the bottom).
4. Roast meat until the center reaches 130° F (30–45 minutes, depending on if you are cooking two smaller tenderloins or one large one). Let meat rest for 10 minutes.
5. While the meat rests, make the Horseradish Cream Sauce, adding horseradish to the mayonnaise, one teaspoon at a time, until you reach your desired level of strength. Season with salt and pepper to taste.
6. Slice meat and serve warm or at room temperature, with horseradish.

FRIED GNOCCHI AGLIO E OLIO

V	Serves 6	Prep Time: 5 minutes	Cook Time: 15 minutes

I will always and forever love the classic Italian dish Spaghetti Aglio e Olio. I will always and forever love my version, with fried gnocchi, even more. On its own it makes a fantastic vegetarian main course, but you can also add cannellini beans to punch up the protein . . . or sausage to make it acceptable to meat lovers.

2 pounds potato gnocchi

4 tablespoons extra virgin olive oil

4 tablespoons salted butter

2 garlic cloves, smashed

1 teaspoon crushed red pepper flakes (optional)

1/4 cup parsley, chopped

1/4 cup basil, chopped

1/2 cup freshly grated pecorino-Romano or Parmesan cheese

salt to taste

1. Prep herbs and garlic.
2. In a large frying pan, heat half the butter and half the oil, until butter is melted. Add crushed garlic to butter and oil, and toast until it reaches a golden brown. Remove garlic from oil and set aside.
3. To the oil, add crushed red pepper flakes (if using) and toast until fragrant (30–60 seconds).
4. Working in batches, add half the gnocchi to pan in a single layer. Fry in butter and oil until the gnocchi become lightly brown and slightly crisp (about 7–10 minutes). Transfer to a warm baking dish, cover, then repeat the process with the remaining butter, oil, garlic, crushed red pepper flakes and gnocchi.
5. When the second batch of gnocchi is golden brown, return the first batch to the pan.
6. Toss in herbs, cheese (and diced fried garlic if you like); check for salt and add if needed.
7. Divide evenly onto plates and serve.

COUSCOUS WITH SAUSAGE & CURRY

Serves 10–12	Prep Time: 5 minutes	Cook Time: 20 minutes

This dish is not even close to authentic Middle Eastern cuisine. Combining sausage and curry is something Middle Eastern cultures just don't do, with both Jewish and Islamic dietary laws forbidding the consumption of pork. But it is something I absolutely do in my Catholic kitchen, where I decided that sausage and curry (and feta and pistachios) really need to go with each other.

- 4 cups uncooked couscous
- 6 tablespoons curry powder
- 2 pounds pork sausage (or sweet Italian sausage), loose or with casings removed
- 8 ounces feta
- 2 yellow onions, chopped
- 2 cups raisins
- 2 cups pistachios, shelled and roughly chopped
- extra virgin olive oil
- 1 bunch cilantro or parsley, chopped
- salt and pepper to taste

1. Heat 2 tablespoons of olive oil in a heavy-bottomed pan. Add sausage, onion, and 2 tablespoons of curry powder. Brown until cooked through.
2. While sausage cooks, cook couscous according to package directions, adding remaining curry powder when you add couscous to the water.
3. When couscous has absorbed the water, add it to the sausage and onion mixture. Stir, then add pistachios. Check seasonings, adding salt and pepper to taste.
4. Drizzle with olive oil and toss. Add feta and raisins.
5. Garnish with cilantro or parsley and serve immediately or at room temperature.

ROASTED CHICKEN

GF, DF, NF	Serves 6	Prep Time: 15 minutes	Cook Time: 90 minute + 15 minutes resting

Once, long ago, I bought a whole chicken for reasons I don't entirely recall. Maybe it was on sale? When it came time to cook it, I googled some recipes and settled on Ina Garten's. The only problem was that I didn't have about half the ingredients the recipe called for. So I improvised. It worked. The original Ina Garten recipe may be excellent. But I've never actually tried it. I liked my version so much that I've stuck with it.

1 (5 to 6 pound) whole chicken
2 large bunches fresh oregano
1 lemon, halved
20 garlic cloves, peeled and crushed
2 tablespoons butter, melted
1 large yellow onion, thickly sliced
3 pounds red potatoes, quartered
2 pounds green beans, trimmed
extra virgin olive oil
salt
freshly ground black pepper

1. Preheat the oven to 425° F.
2. Pat the chicken dry with paper towels. Place in a roasting pan or deep-sided baking dish.
3. Salt and pepper the inside of the chicken. Stuff with half the oregano, lemon halves, and all the garlic.
4. Brush the outside of the chicken with the butter and sprinkle with 1 teaspoon salt and 1/2 teaspoon pepper. Tie the legs together with kitchen string.
5. Place the potatoes, onions, and remaining oregano around the chicken. Drizzle liberally with olive oil and toss with 2 teaspoons salt and 1/2 teaspoon pepper.
6. Roast the chicken for 1 hour and 5 minutes, then add green beans to potatoes and onion, tossing to coat with olive oil.
7. Roast for another 25 minutes or until the juices run clear. Remove from oven.
8. Separate the vegetables and cover them with foil to keep warm. Allow chicken to rest for about 15 minutes (I usually rush this part).
9. Slice chicken onto a platter and serve with vegetables.

CAPRESE PASTA

NF	Serves 6	Prep Time: 5 minutes	Cook Time: 20 minutes

This is another family favorite designed around the late summer's abundance of tomatoes and basil and my deep conviction that burrata makes everything better.

1 pound cavatappi pasta

1 pound spicy Italian sausage, loose or with casings removed

4 garlic cloves, minced

24–30 basil leaves

8 ounces burrata, divided into 6 portions

2 cups (16 ounces) cherry tomatoes, halved

1/4 cup extra virgin olive oil

salt and pepper to taste

1. Bring a large pot of salted water to a boil. Add pasta and cook until al dente. Reserve 1 cup of pasta water, then drain.
2. While the pasta cooks, brown sausage in a large, deep-sided pan. Once the sausage is cooked through, add the garlic and continue cooking for about another minute.
3. Add the hot pasta to the sausage. Toss to combine. Remove from heat. Add olive oil, about 1/2 cup of pasta water, and cherry tomatoes (adding more water if pasta seems dry). Add basil and toss to combine.
4. Serve on individual plates, topping with burrata.

HERB-CRUSTED PORK LOIN

GF, DF, NF	Serves: 8	PrepTime: 15 minutes active; 8–24 hours inactive	Cook Time: approximately 1 hour

Feeding meat to a crowd is rarely affordable, but this dish is the exception. Pork loin is both inexpensive and feeds 8 to 10 people with ease. Just make sure to buy pork loin—not pork tenderloin, which is also delicious but much smaller and more expensive.

- 3–4 pounds pork loin
- 4–5 large rosemary sprigs, leaves removed from stem
- 8 garlic cloves
- 1 tablespoon lemon-pepper blend (in spice grinder)
- 1/2 teaspoon salt
- 1/4 tablespoon freshly ground pepper
- 2 tablespoons extra virgin olive oil
- kitchen string

Gravy

- 1/2 tablespoon butter
- 2 tablespoons all-purpose or gluten-free flour
- 1 1/2 cups whole milk
- 2 cups chicken broth
- 2–3 tablespoons sherry
- salt and pepper to taste

1. Mince rosemary, and garlic. Combine in a small dish with the lemon-pepper blend, salt, and pepper.
2. Butterfly pork loin (slicing it through the middle so it opens like a book). Rub half of herb mixture across the inside of the pork.
3. "Close" the loin and tie with kitchen string at the ends and in the middle.
4. Spread the remaining rub across the exterior top of the roast and drizzle with olive oil.
5. Wrap tightly in plastic and refrigerate for 8 hours or overnight.
6. When ready to roast, preheat oven to 350° F.
7. Roast for approximately 1 hour or until the internal temperature reaches 145° F. Remove and allow to rest for 10–15 minutes.
8. While the meat rests, make your gravy. In a small saucepan, melt butter. Add chicken broth and bring to a simmer. In a mason jar, combine flour and milk. Shake until well mixed. Slowly start adding milk and flour mixture to the chicken broth, whisking continuously, until the gravy reaches your desired thickness. Add sherry and season with salt and pepper.
9. Slice pork loin and serve with gravy on the side.

PAN-FRIED GNOCCHI WITH BACON, BRUSSELS SPROUTS, BUTTERNUT SQUASH & BALSAMIC GLAZE

GF*	Serves 6	Prep Time: 15 minutes	Cook Time: 25 minutes

I like pasta. I love gnocchi. Especially fried gnocchi. It's crispy and buttery on the outside, tender and fluffy on the inside, and always comforting on a cold winter's night. This was a favorite of mine and my roommates long ago, and it remains a favorite today, especially when butternut squash season arrives.

If you can find pre-cut squash in your grocery store, buy that and save yourself some prep time. If you can't, frozen butternut squash is also a great time saver. You just need to preheat the pan first, drizzling the pan itself with oil before you put it in the oven, then adding the squash (with more oil and salt) once the pan is sizzling. The preheating prevents the squash from getting too soft.

- 2 pounds gnocchi (gluten-free works well if you need it)
- 4 cups butternut squash , peeled, seeded, and cubed
- 1 pound brussels sprouts
- 1 pound bacon, thick slices if possible
- 10–12 fresh sage leaves
- 1/4 cup pumpkin seeds (pepitas)
- salt
- 1/4 cup extra virgin olive oil, divided
- 4 tablespoons butter

Balsamic Glaze

- 1/2 balsamic vinegar
- 1/4 cup sugar

1. Preheat oven to 450° F.
2. While the oven warms, combine vinegar and sugar in a small pot and stir. Bring to a boil. Continue boiling, stirring occasionally, until it is reduced by about half. Remove from heat and set aside.
3. While the glaze reduces, trim ends off brussels sprouts and cut in half lengthwise.
4. When the oven is hot, arrange the squash on one parchment-lined baking sheet and the brussels sprouts, flat side down, on another. Drizzle both with olive oil and salt. Roast for 20 minutes or until sprouts are browned and the bottoms have begun to caramelize.

(*continued on next page* ⇨)

5. While the vegetable cook, fry the bacon, drain, roughly chop, and set aside.
6. In a large frying pan, combine 2 tablespoons of butter and 2 tablespoons of olive oil. Heat until the butter melts and begins to brown. Arrange one package of the gnocchi in a single layer in the frying pan. Continue cooking (flipping and tossing the gnocchi occasionally) until the gnocchi is golden all over and has a slight crunch to the bite (about 5–6 minutes). Remove to a paper towel and cover with foil to keep warm. Add more butter and oil to the pan and repeat with the second package of gnocchi.
7. In the last minute or so of cooking the second batch of gnocchi, toss in whole sage leaves and allow them to fry with the gnocchi.
8. The vegetables should finish roasting right as the gnocchi finishes frying. Remove the gnocchi from the heat, remove the vegetables from the oven, and combine the squash, brussels sprouts, bacon, gnocchi, and pumpkin seeds together in a large serving bowl. Toss together with the remaining olive oil.
9. Divide the gnocchi evenly on plates and serve with a drizzle of the balsamic glaze.

VEGGIE ENCHILADA BOWLS WITH AVOCADO CREMA

GF, DF, V, VG, NF	Serves 8	Prep Time: 20 minutes	Cook Time: 40 minutes

This recipe was first concocted for a friend fighting cancer (and eating vegan to do so). Our carnivorous, dairy-loving house still happily eats it, though, as do our carnivorous, dairy-loving friends.

Veggie Bowls

- 4 cups uncooked rice
- 2 tablespoons avocado oil
- 2 large yellow onions, chopped
- 4 garlic cloves, minced
- 2 sweet potatoes, peeled and chopped
- 1 red bell pepper, seeded and chopped
- 4 cups fresh spinach, roughly chopped
- 2 (14 ounce) cans black beans, drained and rinsed
- 4 (10 ounce) cans enchilada sauce
- 3 teaspoons ground cumin
- 1 teaspoon garlic powder
- 2 teaspoons chili powder
- 1 lime, juiced
- 1 teaspoon salt
- 1 bunch cilantro, chopped
- 2 cups shredded cheddar cheese (omit for vegan, dairy-free option)
- Avocado Crema (see p. 108)

1. Cook rice according to package directions and keep warm.
2. Boil a small pot of water. Cook sweet potato for about 5–10 minutes until just tender. Drain and set aside.
3. In a large skillet or pot, heat 2 tablespoons of avocado oil over medium heat. Add onion and cook for about 7 minutes, stirring frequently. Add garlic and cook until fragrant (30 seconds–1 minute).
4. Add the sliced peppers, sweet potatoes, black beans, and spinach. Cook on medium heat for 5–7 minutes more.
5. Stir in enchilada sauce, cumin, lime juice, salt, garlic powder, and chili powder. Cook for a minute or two more, until all the flavors are blended. Taste and adjust seasonings if necessary. Keep warm.
6. While veggies cook, make the avocado crema.
7. When ready to serve, fill bowls with rice and top with veggie mixture, avocado crema, and cheese (for the non-vegan, dairy loving-people also eating at your table).

RIGATONI ALL'AMATRICIANA

NF	Serves 6	Prep Time: 5 minutes	Cook Time: 25 minutes

One of the best things about traveling to Rome with small children is that no matter where you go to eat, you will always find some kind of pasta cooked in Amatriciana sauce. It's simple, delectable, and about as kid friendly as food comes. During the two weeks my family spent there in 2024, my children ate it almost every day. At home, they get it less often, but when they do, this is the recipe I use. It is almost, but not quite, a dead ringer for the Rigatoni all' Amatriciana served in my favorite corner of Trastevere and just as much of a kid pleaser as the versions they ate in Rome.

1 pound rigatoni

1 pound bacon

1 small onion, halved and thinly sliced

1 (16 ounce) can whole San Marzano tomatoes

1 cup freshly grated pecorino-Romano cheese

extra virgin olive oil

salt to taste

1. Bring a large pot of well salted water to a boil. Add rigatoni and cook until al dente.
2. While the pasta is cooking, fry the bacon and sliced onion in a large frying pan over medium-high heat until the bacon is fully cooked but not crisp and the onion is soft and translucent.
3. Drain about half the grease from the pan, leaving the bacon, onion, and a few tablespoons of bacon grease behind.
4. To the bacon and onion, add the can of tomatoes and simmer for about five minutes.
5. Add 1/4 cup of pecorino to the tomatoes and stir until it melts into the sauce.
6. When the pasta is done, reserve about a cup of water, then drain (leaving some water clinging to the pasta).
7. Immediately, add the pasta to the sauce, stirring in another 1/4 cup of pecorino.
8. If the sauce seems too thick, add a small bit of reserved water to reach desired consistency.
9. Serve immediately, with the remaining pecorino sprinkled over it.

GARLIC SHRIMP & SPANISH POTATOES

GF, DF, NF	Serves 6	Prep Time: 15 minutes	Cook Time: 25 minutes

Most Fridays, we try to eat meatless. When it's just the five of us, I keep it simple with soup (or take-out pizza). But when we're having guests, this pseudo-Spanish recipe is always a hit.

2 orange or yellow peppers, cored and sliced

2 red peppers, cored and sliced

2 pounds red potatoes, cubed

1 large red onion, halved and sliced

4 garlic cloves, minced

2 pounds uncooked medium or large shrimp, peeled and deveined

1 tablespoon smoked Spanish paprika

1 teaspoon cumin

1 teaspoon ancho chili powder

1 teaspoon harissa seasoning

1/4 teaspoon cayenne pepper

1 bunch chives, chopped

extra virgin olive oil

salt and pepper to taste

1. Preheat oven to 450° F.
2. In a small bowl, mix paprika, cumin, chili powder, harissa, and cayenne; set aside.
3. On a paper towel-lined plate, dry shrimp, then season with salt and pepper; set aside.
4. In a large bowl, combine potatoes with 3 tablespoons olive oil, half of the spice mixture, and desired amount of salt and pepper. Toss to coat, then spread out on a parchment-lined baking sheet. Roast for 20–22 minutes (tossing midway through) or until potatoes are soft and golden.
5. While the potatoes cook, heat 2 tablespoons of olive oil in a large skillet. Add onions and a pinch of salt. Cook until they begin to soften and brown (5 minutes). Add peppers and half the remaining spice mixture and continue cooking until they are soft and starting to brown (8 minutes). Taste for seasoning, adding salt and pepper if desired. Transfer to a large bowl and cover to keep warm.
6. In the same pan, heat another 2 tablespoons of olive oil. Add shrimp and cook for two to three minutes without stirring. Add garlic and remaining seasoning. Cook another one to two minutes until shrimp are pink and cooked through. Remove from heat.
7. In a large bowl, combine shrimp, peppers, and potatoes. Toss well, then plate.
8. Serve topped with chopped chives (or parsley or cilantro).

TORTELLINI WITH ROMESCO SAUCE

Serves 6	Prep Time: 5 minutes	Cook Time: 15 minutes

32 ounces cheese tortellini

Romesco Sauce

1 (12 ounce) jar roasted red peppers (such as Cento), drained

1/2 cup raw almonds

1/4 cup sun-dried tomatoes, oil packed (such as Mezzetta or Alessi)

2 large garlic cloves

1 tablespoon red wine vinegar

1 teaspoon chili powder

1/4 teaspoon cayenne pepper

1/2 cup extra virgin olive oil

1/2 teaspoon salt

1/4 cup chopped parsley

1. Bring a large pot of salted water to boil. Add tortellini and cook according to package directions. Drain and return to pot.
2. While the water boils, combine all the ingredients except for the olive oil and parsley, in a blender; begin blending. Once the ingredients are well combined, slowly pour in the olive oil and continue to blend until the sauce is smooth and creamy.
3. You will have roughly 1 1/2 cups of romesco sauce when done. Set aside 1 cup for this recipe, then freeze the remainder to use in recipes such as Oven-Baked Gnocchi with Sausage (see p. 198) or Oven-Baked Gnocchi with Feta and Tomatoes (see p. 209).
4. Toss the tortellini and romesco sauce together, top with parsley, and serve.

CHANA MASALA

GF, DF*, V*, VG*, NF	Serves 8	Prep Time: 10 minutes	Cook Time: 20 minutes

In college, one of my best friend's parents were from India. They also were amazing cooks who, during finals week, took pity on their overly studious daughter (and her overly studious friends) and would bring us giant Tupperware containers full of chana masala. It made finals (almost) something to look forward to. In all my years of trying, I've never managed to replicate the absolute deliciousness of their chana masala. This recipe is as close as I've gotten.

Be warned: This is definitely on the spicy side. You can minimize the spiciness by adding less cayenne and fewer peppers. I make the recipe as is for my family but serve the kids' portions with an abundance of the yogurt cooling sauce.

Chana Masala

4 tablespoons ghee (or coconut oil for dairy-free or vegan option)

2 medium yellow onions, diced

8 garlic cloves, minced

3 jalapeño peppers, seeded and minced

4 inches fresh ginger, peeled and minced

2 tablespoons ground coriander

2 teaspoons cumin

2 teaspoons salt

1 teaspoon cayenne pepper

2 teaspoons turmeric

2 (15 ounce) cans diced tomatoes

6 tablespoons tomato paste

4 (15 ounce) cans chickpeas, drained and rinsed

2 teaspoons garam masala

Cooling Sauce

1 cup plain Greek yogurt

1/2 teaspoon garlic

1 tablespoon extra virgin olive oil

For Serving

cooked jasmine rice

1 small bunch cilantro, chopped

naan or other flatbread

1. In a large heavy-bottomed pot, melt the ghee. Add the onions and cook for about 10 minutes on medium low heat, or until they are just beginning to caramelize. Add all but 1/2 teaspoon of the garlic, plus all of the ginger and jalapeno. Stir.
2. Cook for about two minutes, then add tomato paste and stir well. Spread out tomato mixture as evenly as possible in one layer across the pot, and turn up the heat to high. Cook for 2–3 minutes or until a brown crust begins to form on the bottom.
3. Add the coriander, cumin, cayenne, salt, and turmeric to tomato mixture and stir well.

(continued on next page ⇨)

4. Add diced tomatoes, using the liquid to deglaze the pan. Then add chickpeas and Garam Masala. Cook for about five minutes or until the chickpeas have heated through.
5. Keep warm on stove until ready to serve.
6. To make your cooling sauce, mix together yogurt, remaining garlic, and olive oil. Slowly add water, 1 tablespoon at a time, until sauce is thinned. Season with salt and pepper to taste.
7. Serve on top of rice or with naan and with a dollop of cooling sauce and cilantro.

Blood Oranges in the Snow

This cocktail takes its name from my favorite Christmas album by my favorite band (Over the Rhine) and tastes a bit like a Manhattan, only sweeter.

1 1/2 ounces bourbon

1/2 ounce cherry liquor

1/2 ounce orange juice, freshly squeezed (it doesn't have to be a blood orange, but it's extra fun if it is)

2–3 dashes Angostura Bitters

1 orange slice

1. Fill a large cocktail shaker with ice.
2. Combine bourbon, cherry liquor, orange juice, and bitters. Shake while saying one Hail Mary.

NANA'S LASAGNA

NF	Serves 8	Prep Time: 90 minutes	Cook Time: 45 minutes

A solid half of what I know about easy hospitality, I learned from one of my mom's best friends, Aunt Linda ("Nana" to her grandchildren, my children, and all my nieces and nephews). We practically lived at her house when we were little, and whether we were eating take-out pizza or dining on her Italian-born grandparents' recipes, the parties would always last late into the night, with the kids staying as far away from the adults as possible. By our choice, mind you. We hoped that if they didn't see us, they would forget entirely about our bedtimes and let us play as long as we liked. They usually did.

2 pounds ground beef
1 large yellow onion, chopped
1 bay leaf
1 garlic clove, crushed
1/4 cup sugar
1 (28 ounce) can Italian tomatoes
2 carrots, shredded
1 (6 ounce) can tomato paste
1 (16 ounce) box lasagna noodles
1/4 cup water
1/4 cup chopped fresh parsley
4 tablespoons chopped fresh basil
2 tablespoons chopped fresh oregano
2 teaspoons salt
2 cups or 1 (15 ounce) tub ricotta cheese
32 ounces mozzarella cheese, shredded
1/4 cup shredded Parmesan cheese
extra virgin olive oil

1. Preheat oven to 350° F.
2. In a large pot, heat 2 tablespoons of olive oil. Add onion and a pinch of salt and cook until soft and translucent (3–5 minutes). Add garlic and cook 30 seconds to 1 minute more.
3. Add beef to the onions and garlic, and brown well. Drain grease and return to pot.
4. To the meat mixture, add tomatoes, tomato paste, carrots, water, and salt.
5. Heat to boiling, then reduce heat and simmer for at least one hour, stirring often. A few minutes before removing from the heat, stir in fresh herbs and check to see if the sauce needs more salt.
6. While sauce simmers, heat a large pot of water to boiling. Add olive oil and salt, then slowly slide in noodles a few at a time. Cook till al dente. Drain and dry on paper towels.
7. To assemble the lasagna: line bottom of lightly oiled baking dish with noodles, 1/3 sauce (bay leaf removed), 1/3 ricotta, 1/3 mozzarella, 1/3 Parmesan. Repeat for three layers.
8. Bake for 30–45 minutes or until bubbly.
9. Serve immediately or cover dish with foil and keep warm until ready to eat.

BARBECUED BEEF BRISKET

GF, DF, NF	Serves 10	Prep Time: 10 minutes active; 8 hours inactive	Cook Time: 11 hours

Having lived with women from Texas, Arkansas, Tennessee, and Oklahoma, I have developed a great respect for the varieties of barbecued brisket from each of those fair states. I use the recipe that came from the Oklahoma roommate, though.

For the barbecue sauce, I prefer to make my own. I love Martha Stewart's Five Ingredient barbecue sauce recipe. It takes 10 minutes, and I always have the ingredients on hand. Primal Kitchen, however, is a solid option if you are looking for something low sugar and without seed oils.

- 10 pounds brisket, untrimmed
- 3 tablespoons Worcestershire sauce
- 3 tablespoons liquid smoke
- 6 teaspoons fajita seasoning
- 2 teaspoons garlic salt
- 24 ounces good quality barbecue sauce

1. Rub brisket with garlic salt and fajita seasoning. Place the brisket fat side up in a large, oven safe baking dish or roasting pan and pour liquids over the meat. Cover tightly and place in fridge overnight.
2. Early the next morning, preheat oven to 250° F.
3. Bake, covered with foil, for 10 hours.
4. After 10 hours, the meat should pull apart easily with a fork. At that point, remove brisket from oven. Drain liquid from pan, then shred meat, removing fat as you go.
5. Return the meat to the pan, cover with 16 ounces of barbecue sauce, and bake one hour more, uncovered.
6. Serve with remaining barbecue sauce, either as sandwiches or on top of Garlic Mashed Potatoes (p. 219) or, as pictured here, Cauliflower Mash (p. 231).

BACON CARBONARA

NF	Serves 6	Prep Time: 5 minutes	Cook Time: 20 minutes

Yes, I know, the proper meat for carbonara is guanciale, not bacon. Unfortunately, they don't carry guanciale at the local ALDI. So when my friend Stephanie shared a recipe for carbonara that involved bacon, I made it the first chance I got. In the years since, I have made a variation of her recipe at least three dozen times. Mine comes with a little more sauce and a lot more bacon. It also calls for a thicker pasta (better to soak up the sauce). It is always on the monthly dinner rotation and a huge hit with my own and my friends' kids.

1 pound bacon (preferably thick cut)
2 garlic cloves, peeled
1 pound bucatini (or fettuccine or linguine)
3 large eggs
1 cup grated Parmesan cheese, plus extra for serving
salt and pepper to taste
crushed red pepper flakes (optional)

1. Bring a large pot of very salty water to a boil (it should taste like sea water).
2. While the water is heating, chop uncooked bacon into bite-sized pieces.
3. Add bacon to a large frying pan, along with the 2 cloves of garlic, and cook until bacon is just shy of crisp. Drain bacon, making sure you reserve half the grease for the pasta.
4. In a large bowl, combine 3 raw eggs (beaten), Parmesan, bacon, and the remainder of the bacon grease.
5. Once the water is boiling, add pasta and cook until al dente (firm to the bite, but not hard). Drain.
6. Immediately, while the pasta is hot, transfer it to the large bowl with eggs, cheese, and bacon. Toss to thoroughly combine, making sure the pasta is evenly coated with the egg and bacon sauce.
7. Generously add pepper to taste (I usually do 20–30 turns of the peppermill).
8. Serve hot, with more freshly grated Parmesan and crushed red pepper if desired.

OVEN-BAKED GNOCCHI WITH SAUSAGE

GF*	Serves 6	Prep Time: 10 minutes	Cook Time: 40–45 minutes

This is a Blue Apron knockoff. When we first tried the dish through the meal prep delivery service, I was ecstatic about how little time it took to throw this together (plus the ease of using just one dish in meal prep). The recipe as I make it now, with homemade romesco sauce, is a bit different from the original, but just as tasty and almost as quick, making it a favorite on nights when I have zero time to cook and just need to get dinner in the oven ASAP.

- 1 1/2 pounds Italian sausage, loose or with casings removed
- 2 pounds gnocchi (gluten-free if needed)
- 1 (6 ounce) can tomato paste
- 1 cup heavy cream
- 1/2 cup Parmesan cheese
- 1/2 cup romesco sauce (see recipe on p. 188)
- 1 teaspoon dried rosemary
- 1 teaspoon dried sage
- 1 teaspoon dried fennel

1. Preheat oven to 450° F.
2. Make the Romesco Sauce according to direction on page 188.
3. In a large bowl, combine tomato paste, heavy cream, romesco sauce, dried herbs, and 1 1/2 cups of water. Add gnocchi to the bowl and stir until combined.
4. Transfer gnocchi mixture to a 9 x 13-inch (or similarly sized) baking dish. Using your hands, tear the sausage into bite-sized pieces and layer on top of the gnocchi.
5. Cover tightly with foil and bake for 45 minutes or until the sausage is cooked through.
6. Serve with Parmesan cheese.

VODKA SAUCE

GF, NF	Serves 8	Prep Time: 10 minutes	Cook Time: 60 minutes

Years ago, I had way too much vodka left over from a party. Not being a vodka drinker, I wasn't sure what to do with it. Someone suggested vodka sauce. I googled, found a recipe, tinkered as is my wont, and the result was this.

Traditionally vodka sauce is served over spaghetti, but I prefer something nice and wide that really catches lots of the sauce (like rigatoni or penne). To serve to a gluten-free crowd, you can always use some form of gluten-free pasta, but creamy polenta (see p. 215) is also a delicious option.

- 1 pound Italian sausage, loose or with casings removed
- 2 large onions, chopped
- 1 1/2 teaspoons salt
- 1/4 teaspoon crushed red pepper flakes
- 14 garlic cloves, minced
- 1 (28 ounce) can crushed tomatoes
- 1 1/2 cups vodka
- 1 cup heavy cream
- 1 cup fresh basil, chopped
- 1/2 cup grated Parmesan cheese
- 4 tablespoons extra virgin olive oil

1. In a large pot, heat the olive oil; add the sausage and cook, until browned.
2. Add onion, salt, and red pepper flakes, stirring frequently. Until the onions are golden. Add the garlic and cook until fragrant, about 30 seconds. Add the tomatoes and cook until the sauce begins to thicken (about 10 minutes).
3. Add the vodka and cook until the sauce is reduced by half (20–30 minutes minutes).
4. Stir in the cream and heat through.
5. Keep warm on the stove until ready to serve. Immediately before serving, stir in the basil and check for seasonings, adding salt or crushed red pepper flakes as necessary. Serve with freshly grated Parmesan.

CHORIZO, BEAN & CORN BOWLS

GF, NF	Serves 6	Prep Time: 5 Minutes	Cook Time: 25 Minutes

If you are a busy mom, with zero time or energy to cook, this recipe is for you. It requires only 5 minutes of prep and bakes in 25 minutes. It has been a lifesaver for me on many a night, and I hope it is for you too.

2 cups uncooked rice

1 pound chorizo sausage

2 (15 ounce) cans black beans, drained and rinsed

2 (15 ounce) cans corn, drained

8 ounces cherry tomatoes

4 tablespoons tomato paste

1 1/2 cups shredded cheddar

Toppings

guacamole

sour cream

jalapeños

1. Preheat the oven to 450° F.
2. On the stove or in a rice cooker, cook rice according to package directions.
3. In a large oven-safe pan (8.5 x 11-inch or the equivalent), mix together beans, corn, cherry tomatoes, and tomato paste, with 1/4 cup of water.
4. Tear uncooked chorizo into bite-sized pieces and scatter on top of beans and corn mixture.
5. Bake uncovered for 25 minutes (or until Chorizo is cooked through). During the last five minutes of cooking, remove Chorizo from oven and scatter cheese on top.
6. When the cheese has melted, remove from oven. Serve on top of rice, and top with guacamole, sour cream, and jalapenos if desired.

BAKED TORTELLINI WITH PESTO

V	Serves 8	Prep Time: 20 minutes	Bake Time: 25 minutes

Many Christmases ago, I got sucked into a debate on Facebook. Like all Facebook debates, it was pointless. To make matters worse, it was the day my husband's entire office was coming to our house for their annual Christmas luncheon. Fortunately, I was making the fastest and easiest of fancy dishes in my recipe box. Twenty minutes prep, twenty-five minutes more in the oven, and no one was any the wiser about my little Facebook distraction.

2 (20 ounce) bags frozen tortellini

8 ounces pesto

6 ounces sun-dried tomatoes in oil (such as Mezzetta or Alessi), drained and sliced

1/2 cup pine nuts

1 (15 ounce) can sliced black olives

8 ounces sliced provolone

1. Preheat the oven to 350° F.
2. In a medium-sized frying pan, lightly toast pine nuts over medium heat. When they begin to release their aroma and brown ever so slightly, remove from pan and set aside.
3. Bring a large pot of salted water to boil. Once the water is boiling, add tortellini and cook according to package instructions.
4. Once the tortellini is cooked, drain and place tortellini in a large bowl.
5. Stir in pesto, sun-dried tomatoes, olives, and pine nuts.
6. Pour into an extra-large baking dish (11 x 15-inch or similar). Top with sliced provolone. Then either refrigerate until ready to cook or bake for 25–30 minutes until the cheese has melted.

MUSHROOM RAVIOLI WITH SAGE CREAM SAUCE

NF	Serves: 6	Prep Time: 5 minutes	Cook Time: 20

2 (20 ounce) bags mushroom ravioli (I use ALDI's Priano brand)

1 yellow onion, minced

8 ounces pancetta, diced

2/3 cup chicken broth

1/2 cup white wine

3 tablespoons butter

1/2 cup heavy cream

2 tablespoons chopped fresh sage

1 teaspoon herbes de Provence

1/2 cup grated Parmesan cheese

extra virgin olive oil

salt and pepper to taste

1. Fill a medium-sized pot halfway with water, salt generously, and bring to a boil. Add ravioli and cook 5–7 minutes or until tender. Drain; return to the pot. Drizzle lightly with olive oil to prevent sticking. Cover to keep warm.
2. Meanwhile, chop onion and sage. Then, in a large, deep-sided skillet, heat 2 tablespoons of olive oil. Add onion, with a pinch of salt and pepper, and cook until golden (5 minutes).
3. Add pancetta and cook until it begins to crisp (5 minutes more). Remove from pan and cover to keep warm.
4. Keeping the heat at medium-hot, add chicken broth and wine to the pan. Deglaze, scraping up any browned bits from the bottom with a spatula. Cook for about one minute.
5. Add the cream, sage, and herbes de Provence to the wine and broth. Cook until heated through (about 2 minutes).
6. Add pancetta and onions back into the sauce. Stir, then add Parmesan. Check for seasonings, adding salt and pepper if necessary. Add ravioli to pan and toss to coat.
7. Serve immediately, topping with additional Parmesan if desired.

OVEN-BAKED GNOCCHI WITH FETA & TOMATOES

GF*, V	Serves 6	Prep Time: 5 minutes	Cook Time: 40 minutes

Do you remember the viral baked feta dip that was all the rage on TikTok a while back? This is my entrée version of that dip.

- 3 pounds gnocchi (gluten-free if needed)
- 4 (8 ounce) cans tomato sauce
- 1 cup heavy cream
- 1/2 cup romesco sauce (store-bought or see recipe on p. 188)
- 8 garlic cloves, peeled and smashed
- 2 cups (16 ounces) cherry tomatoes
- 1 (8 ounce) block feta
- 1 cup basil, roughly chopped
- 1/2 cup grated Parmesan cheese
- salt and pepper to taste

1. Preheat the oven to 450° F.
2. In a large bowl, combine tomato sauce, cream, romesco sauce, one teaspoon of salt, and a 1/4 teaspoon of pepper. Add in garlic, tomatoes, and gnocchi. Stir until gnocchi is coated.
3. Transfer gnocchi mixture to an extra-large baking dish (11 x 15-inch or similar). Distribute evenly throughout the dish. Cover tightly with foil and bake for 30 minutes.
4. Remove pan from oven and uncover. Nestle the block of feta into the center of the gnocchi, then return the pan to the oven and bake, uncovered, for 10 minutes more.
5. Remove from oven and scatter chopped basil across the gnocchi.
6. Serve with a sprinkling of Parmesan.

PRACTICAL HOSPITALITY

Working with What You Have

These days, my family and I call a rambling old Arts and Crafts house, "home." It's spacious inside and out, with three floors full of large and gracious rooms and a big, shaded yard, fenced in to protect the little ones. (It's also situated in one of the poorest neighborhoods in the state of Ohio, which is how a Catholic school teacher and Catholic writer can afford it.)

For us, it is easy to host a crowd. I routinely invite my children's whole preschool over for a playdate in the backyard without thinking about it. But I know it's not that easy for most people. No matter how much you may want to host, space constrictions (or budget constrictions) can leave you feeling like everyday hospitality (or any kind of hospitality) is beyond your reach.

It doesn't have to be out of your reach though. Not everyone has the space to host or the money to feed a crowd, but everybody can practice hospitality. You don't need a well-funded bank account or even a home to obey the biblical command to be hospitable; you just need to have a heart open to others. You can start by . . .

1. Inviting a single friend or an elderly neighbor to join your family for a weeknight supper.
2. Making a meal or a treat for a new family in the parish or the neighborhood.
3. Inviting friends to bring sack lunches and meet up at the park.
4. Coordinating a potluck dinner at your parish after feast day Masses or on Fridays in Lent.
5. Throwing a soup and bread party, where every family signs up to bring either soup, bread, or wine; host this at your home if you have room or at a local parish if not.
6. Inviting friends over for dessert on the porch on a Sunday afternoon.
7. Inviting a single friend to join you and your family at church on Sunday and grabbing coffee together afterward.
8. Planning a meetup at a local coffee shop.
9. Coordinating a tailgate party before a local game or free concert in the park.
10. Going on a Sunday hike and inviting friends or another family along.

SIDES

Most of the time, when hosting, there's no need to make a side dish. A simple salad, either prepared by you or brought by a guest, goes well with just about anything. Easy roasted veggies are also a quick option. Every once in a while, though, especially on holidays, the occasion calls for a little something more. These are the very best of my "more."

CREAMY POLENTA

GF, V, NF	Serves 8	Prep Time: 2 minutes	Cook Time: 15 minutes

I'm sure this recipe is going to give some poor Italian grandmother fits, but trust me, it will make you happy. It makes almost everyone happy. Small children love it. Men love it. Heck, even my pure-blooded Italian friends love it. It tastes better than any polenta you will ever eat in any American restaurant, and almost as good as the polenta they serve at the Taverna di Mercanti in Rome. Almost.

- 6 cups chicken broth
- 1 cup heavy cream (half-and-half or whole milk will work too)
- 1 1/2 cups instant polenta
- 1 cup grated Parmesan cheese
- 4 tablespoons butter
- 1 1/2–2 teaspoons salt

1. Bring chicken broth and cream to a boil over medium-high heat in a large, heavy-bottomed pot, stirring occasionally to prevent cream from scalding.
2. Once the liquid is boiling, very slowly pour in the polenta, stirring constantly as you pour.
3. Once the polenta has thickened to the point that it starts pulling away from the side of the pot (about 5 minutes), remove from heat and stir in butter, Parmesan, and 1 1/2 teaspoons of salt.
4. Taste and add a touch more salt if necessary (it almost always is for me). Serve immediately or keep warm in a crockpot until ready to serve . . . but know that the longer it sits, the thicker and less creamy it will get.

GARLIC ROASTED TOMATOES

GF, DF, V, NF, Vegan	Serves 8	Prep Time: 5 minutes	Cook Time: 40 minutes

Fresh tomatoes, with a dash of salt, are a glorious thing. But so are roasted tomatoes, glistening with olive oil and infused with garlic. Pair these with the creamy polenta on page 215 for a simple and delicious Friday night supper or serve them on their own with chicken, sausage, or any grilled meat.

- 10–12 large Roma tomatoes
- 6 garlic cloves, peeled and smashed
- 1/4 cup extra virgin olive oil
- 4 tablespoons roughly chopped basil
- salt and pepper to taste

1. Preheat oven to 400° F; line a large baking tray with parchment paper.
2. Trim the tops off the tomatoes and slice in half lengthwise.
3. Arrange tomatoes and smashed garlic on the same pan. Drizzle with olive oil and sprinkle liberally with salt and pepper.
4. Roast for 40 minutes.
5. Remove from oven and transfer to serving platter. Sprinkle with fresh basil and serve.

GARLIC MASHED POTATOES

GF, V, NF	Serves 8	Prep Time: 20 minutes	Cook Time: 40 minutes

These are very special potatoes (repeat: very special potatoes), made on very special occasions. Accordingly, none of the fat or calories count. So don't even let yourself think about it when making these. Add dairy with abandon and give praise to God for the cow. Also save yourself some stress and make these several hours before you eat. Then keep them warm in a crockpot (set on warm) until dinnertime, stirring occasionally to prevent browning. (I usually leave mine in there for about 4 hours.)

5 pounds red, yellow, or russet potatoes, skins on or peeled

1 (8 ounce) block cream cheese, at room temperature

1 head garlic

1 teaspoon extra virgin olive oil

4 tablespoons butter, at room temperature

1 cup heavy cream

1 cup whole milk

salt and pepper to taste

1. Preheat oven to 400° F. Peel the outer layer of skin off the garlic, trim the top off it, drizzle with olive oil, and wrap in foil. Roast for 40 minutes (while peeling and boiling the potatoes). When soft, set aside and open up the foil so the garlic can cool.
2. Wash and cube potatoes. In a large pot, (just) cover them with cold water, and bring to a boil. When the potatoes fall apart at the touch of a fork (approximately 15 minutes), remove from heat and drain.
3. In a large mixing bowl, thoroughly mash the potatoes. Next, add in the cream cheese, butter, and roasted garlic (skin completely removed). Whip using a hand or stand mixer.
4. Slowly add in cream. If the potatoes seem too thick, slowly add milk until you reach your desired consistency.
5. Add salt and pepper to taste. (Note: whipped potatoes need a healthy amount of salt to be worth their salt, so don't be afraid here. I use about two to three teaspoons of salt when I make mine. I start with two teaspoons, then add by the 1/2 teaspoon until I'm happy.)
6. Keep warm in crock-pot until ready to serve.

THANKSGIVING BRUSSELS SPROUTS

GF, DF	Serves 8	Prep Time: 15 minutes	Cook Time: 25 minutes

Most of the people who eat at my house are obsessed with brussels sprouts. They are comfort food to us. Which sounds like crazy talk until you eat them, all caramelized, infused with garlic and oil, and completely delicious. This version, however, takes our favorite vegetable to a whole new level. We serve them at Thanksgiving and Christmas, but you can serve them anytime you like.

Tip: When cooking for a major holiday, I cut up all the veggies the night before or morning of, and cook the bacon before guests come, keeping it warm under foil. Before anyone shows up, I get all the veggies on trays, and then, 30 minutes before we eat, pop it into a preheated oven so it can be served hot and fresh.

- 1 pound brussels sprouts
- 3 cups butternut squash, peeled, seeded, and cubed
- 10 garlic cloves, peeled and smashed
- 5–6 bacon slices
- 1/2 cup pecans
- 4 tablespoons extra virgin olive oil
- salt and pepper to taste

1. Preheat oven to 400° F.
2. Trim the stems off the brussels sprouts, then cut each one in half lengthwise. Set aside until ready to use.
3. On the stovetop, fry the bacon. Drain, then crumble the bacon into bite-sized pieces.
4. Line a large sheet pan with parchment paper. Spread out the squash, sprouts (flat side down), and garlic cloves. Drizzle vegetables with 4 tablespoons of olive oil and 1–2 teaspoons of salt.
5. Roast vegetables for 25–30 minutes (until the sprouts are caramelized on the bottom), adding the pecans to the pan in the last several minutes of cooking.
6. In a serving dish, combine the vegetables with the bacon. Toss and serve immediately.

ROASTED CURRIED CAULIFLOWER

GF, DF, V, VG, NF	Serves 8	Prep Time: 10 minutes	Cook Time: 40 minutes

You know those Indian main courses for which I gave you recipes in the last section? This is the side dish that goes with them all. When cooking for company, you can prep everything up to an hour or two ahead of time, and then pop the cauliflower in the oven to roast for half an hour before dinner.

- 2 large heads cauliflower, chopped into medium-sized florets
- 2 tablespoons cumin
- 2 tablespoons curry powder
- 1 tablespoon turmeric
- 2 teaspoons salt
- 1/2 cup extra virgin olive oil

1. Preheat oven to 450° F; line two large baking sheets with parchment paper.
2. In a large mixing bowl, toss all ingredients and then spread on baking sheets.
3. Roast in the preheated oven for 30–35 minutes (tossing once with a spatula, midway through), until cauliflower has caramelized and is a deep rich brown color.
4. Serve hot.

GRUYÈRE POTATO GRATIN

GF, V, NF	Serves 12	Prep Time: 30 minutes	Cook Time: 90 minutes

Some people have an Easter menu that never varies. Not me. Some years I make ham. Other years, it's lamb or salmon or a brunch with egg casseroles and sweet breads. For many years, though, these potatoes were my constant. They pair well with nearly all meats and brunch dishes, and they're special enough to make any meal feel like a feast worthy of our Lord's Resurrection. Hosting bonus: you can prepare these the day before and reheat them before serving.

Tip: If making this a day early, refrigerate the potatoes after baking. Then, the next day, remove from refrigerator and bring to room temperature before broiling.

4 pounds russet potatoes
5 garlic cloves
1 tablespoon butter
2 medium shallots, quartered
2 1/2 cups heavy cream
1 tablespoon salt
1 teaspoon black pepper
1/2 cup grated Gruyère cheese
1/2 cup grated Parmesan
2 tablespoons finely chopped fresh sage
2 tablespoons roughly chopped fresh rosemary

1. Preheat oven to 325° F and butter the inside of a 9 x 13-inch baking dish.
2. Scrub potatoes clean and slice into 1/4-inch rounds (use a mandolin if possible).
3. In a heavy-bottomed pot, over low heat, slowly bring shallots, cream, salt, pepper, and garlic cloves to a simmer. Cook until shallots and garlic are soft (15–20 minutes). Cool for 5 minutes, then using an immersion blender, puree until smooth (alternately, transfer to a blender or food processor).
4. Layer the potatoes in the prepared dish. Pour cream over potatoes, then cover tightly with foil.
5. Bake potatoes until tender, 60–75 minutes. Let cool.
6. Move oven rack to the highest position and turn on the broiler. Remove foil and sprinkle Gruyère, Parmesan, and most of the fresh sage and rosemary over potatoes. Broil until cheese bubbles and the top is golden brown (5–10 minutes), watching closely.
7. Before serving, top with remaining sage and rosemary.

DUKKAH-SPICED ROASTED CARROTS

GF, DF, V, VG	Serves 8	Prep Time: 15 minutes	Cook Time: 25 minutes

For some reason, I always end up with too many carrots in my vegetable drawer. Probably because ALDI only sells them in industrial-sized bags, and many recipes call for only two carrots at a time. This side dish has become one of our favorite ways to use up those carrots and serve our guests something delicious, as well.

Dukkah is a fantastic Egyptian spice blend. Various iterations of dukkah abound, though, so if you have a nut allergy make sure to read the ingredients on the spice package. It is not always nut-free.

12–16 carrots, peeled, halved, and cut into 3-inch sections
4 tablespoons dukkah
4 tablespoons extra virgin olive oil
1 1/2 teaspoons salt

1. Preheat oven to 400° F; line two baking sheets with parchment paper.
2. Toss all ingredients in a large bowl, then spread onto baking sheets.
3. Bake for 25–30 minutes (tossing halfway through cooking), until carrots have caramelized.

ROASTED CAULIFLOWER & GRUYÈRE GALETTE

V, NF	Serves 4–8 as a side	Prep Time: 20 minutes active, 60 minutes inactive	Cook Time: 40 minutes

I do not bake. At least, I do not bake much. But galettes I do. These rustic French tarts require no fancy technical precision. Instead, they allow for improvising. Accordingly, if cauliflower isn't your thing, try making this instead with tomatoes, basil, and mozzarella. Or brussels sprouts, bacon, and the same cheese mixture used on this tart. This is a forgiving crust that tastes great with just about everything. It also goes with just about everything.

Crust

1 1/4 cups flour

1/2 teaspoon sea salt

8 tablespoons cold butter, cut into 1/2-inch pieces

6–7 tablespoons ice cold water

Toppings

1/2 small head cauliflower, cut into bite-sized pieces

1/2 cup grated Gruyère cheese

1/2 cup grated pecorino-Romano cheese

2 ounces fresh mozzarella cheese, sliced

1 handful fresh spinach leaves

1/4 teaspoon crushed red pepper flakes

salt to taste

tablespoons extra virgin olive oil

1. In a medium-sized bowl, combine flour and salt. Cut the butter into the bowl and work it into the flour using your hands (it will be crumbly). Add water, one tablespoon at a time, until a smooth dough forms (be careful not to overwork it). Wrap in plastic wrap and chill in the fridge for at least one hour.
2. While the dough chills, prep your ingredients and preheat oven to 380° F.
3. Roll out the dough on a floured surface into a 10-inch circle. (It does not have to be pretty or perfectly round.) Transfer the dough to a parchment-lined baking sheet.
4. In a separate bowl, toss the cauliflower florets with olive oil and salt to coat.
5. Scatter cheeses, cauliflower, crushed pepper, and spinach onto the crust, leaving about two inches on all sides.
6. Fold in the sides to shape the tart, then pinch the edges with your fingers.
7. Bake for 35–40 minutes or until golden. Serve immediately or at room temperature.

SAUSAGE & APPLE STUFFING

NF	Serves 12	Prep Time: 2 hours	Cook Time: 30 minutes

For over twenty years, this stuffing recipe has been a part of my Thanksgiving dinner. Not a Thanksgiving has gone by when I haven't made it, and it's my most requested recipe from anyone who has every shared a Thanksgiving dinner with us. At least a dozen families now include it in their Thanksgiving Dinner. Please let me know if you end up including it in yours!

I usually start this stuffing on Tuesday night, as the stock takes so long to make. I do the stock then, prepare the stuffing Wednesday, and cook it on Thursday immediately before serving while the turkey is resting.

Turkey Stock

- 6 cups water
- turkey neck and giblets
- 2 celery stalks, sliced into large pieces
- 2 carrots, sliced into large pieces
- 1 large onion, quartered
- 2 tangerines, zested
- 1 bay leaf
- 1 teaspoon whole black peppercorns

Stuffing

- 8 cups (about 1 loaf) white bread, cut into cubes
- 4 cups (about 1/2 loaf) wheat bread, cut into cubes
- 2 pounds pork sausage, loose or with casings removed
- 1 1/2 cups finely chopped celery
- 2 Golden Delicious apples, peeled, cored, and chopped
- 1/2 cup dried cherries
- 1 1/2 cups turkey stock
- 1/2 cup chopped Italian parsley
- 3 tablespoons chopped fresh rosemary
- 2 tablespoons chopped fresh sage
- 2 teaspoons chopped fresh thyme
- 1 cup butter, melted
- 2 tablespoons extra virgin olive oil
- salt and pepper to taste

1. In a large pot, combine the neck, heart, and kidneys, with 6 cups water, celery, carrot, onion, tangerine zest, bay leaf, and peppercorns. Bring to a boil, reduce heat, and simmer for 1 hour, occasionally skimming froth off the top. Add liver and continue to simmer for 30 minutes more. Strain and refrigerate until ready to make stuffing.
2. Preheat oven to 350° F. Arrange the white and whole wheat bread cubes on 2–3 large baking sheets (it's okay if it's crowded; you're drying the bread out, not toasting it). Bake for 7 minutes; transfer to a large bowl.

3. In a large frying pan, heat oil. Add the sausage, onions, and a pinch of salt and pepper. Cook until the sausage is translucent and onion browned.
4. Add the celery and another pinch of salt and pepper. Cook for two minutes more.
5. Pour sausage mixture into the bowl with the bread. Add in chopped apple, dried cherries, and fresh herbs.
6. Add turkey stock and butter. Mix well (hands work best).
7. Spread out onto a large baking pan, keeping a small amount of stuffing for the bird. Cover well and refrigerate (I usually refrigerate overnight).
8. The next day, stuff turkey cavity with reserved stuffing and bake. When the turkey comes out of the oven, set oven temperature to 350° and bake remaining stuffing for 25–30 minutes, while turkey rests and is sliced. Serve immediately.

CAULIFLOWER MASH

GF, V, NF	Serves 8	Prep Time: 5 minutes	Cook Time: 20 minutes

I cannot explain to you how ghee, Parmesan, garlic, and salt can possibly make cauliflower taste so good. It is either some kind of crazy chemistry that my brain cannot grasp or, as my husband says, "magic."

I'm going with magic.

1 large or 2 small heads cauliflower
2 tablespoons ghee
1/2 cup grated Parmesan cheese
4 garlic cloves, peeled
salt and pepper to taste

1. Bring a large pot of salted water to boil. While the water heats, cut cauliflower into medium-sized florets.
2. When the water is boiling, add cauliflower and garlic. Boil until fork tender (about 7–10 minutes).
3. Drain cauliflower, then transfer to a high-powered blender. Puree until smooth, adding ghee and Parmesan (you may have to scrape the sides or tamp the mash down a few times until the cauliflower is more on the pureed side).
4. Season generously with salt and pepper and serve immediately.

PAN-FRIED SUMMER VEGGIES

GF, DF, NF, V, VG	Serves 6	Prep Time: 5 minutes	Cook Time: 10 minutes

I wasn't planning on including this recipe in the cookbook. We eat it at least weekly during the summer months, but it is so simple that I wasn't sure it belonged here. But then, one summer night, as we were sitting down to eat some pasta with this on the side, I glanced down at the bowl, heaping with charred zucchini and tomatoes, and decided to take a picture of it. It was too pretty not to photograph and, as I eventually decided, too delicious not to share here.

2 medium zucchini (about 2 cups when sliced)

16 ounces (2 cups) cherry tomatoes

4 garlic cloves, minced

extra virgin olive oil

salt and pepper to taste

1. Halve the zucchini lengthwise, then slice into 1/4-inch moons.
2. In a large frying pan, heat 2 tablespoons olive oil. When a drop of water sizzles in the pan, arrange zucchini in a single layer (work in batches if necessary, and adding more oil to the pan if it seems dry). Cook over medium-high heat, not stirring for 4 minutes. Add garlic and toss.
3. Cook two minutes more (returning all zucchini to the pan if working in batches) and add tomatoes. Season with salt and pepper. Cook 4–5 minutes more, until tomatoes begin to pop and blister.
4. Serve immediately, adjusting seasoning as needed.

PRACTICAL HOSPITALITY

Feeding Other People's Children

Probably the question I get asked most about hosting large families for dinner is, "But what do you feed the children?"

My short answer is always the same, "I don't."

My long answer is a little more nuanced. I do feed the children. I just don't feed them much.

First, because there is no creature on the planet more fickle about food than a small child. The macaroni and cheese they liked yesterday, they will hate today. The spaghetti sauce they rejected last month, they will gobble up this month. There is never any knowing what will please them, and trying to make a second entrée for children, when it's already taking the last ounce of energy I have to make a first entrée for their parents, is a lesson in thanklessness I don't need.

The second reason I don't go out of my way to cook for small children at parties is because when small children gather, food is the last thing on their mind. Will they graze? Yes. Will they sit down and eat a meal? Usually no. Most will spend the night racing off in ten different directions with the other kids, and it's all most parents can do to get them to eat a slice of cheese.

So that's what I make sure is on hand: grazing food. Cheese, crackers, bread, maybe some deli meat or fruit. Then their parents can toss those things in their general direction as they run by.

If we're doing something simple that kids almost always eat (like pizza), I always have enough for them. If the kids are budding foodies and want to sit down and eat, they can eat what the adults are eating; I always have more than enough of that too. And if the child has food allergies, I'll have something safe on hand for them. But that's the extent of my food accommodations for kids.

Thus far, my friends are on board with this strategy. They know their kids' excitement will outweigh their appetite when other kids are in view. Most parents also want to enjoy their time with their friends when they're out and are happy as clams if the kids stay far, far away during a dinner party. So they feed them a snack before leaving home then let them run feral once they get to my house. It works for us, and the children continue to thrive, despite the occasional dinner of cheese and cake.

DESSERTS

Someone once asked me what is my favorite dessert to serve to company. I told them, "Whatever the company is bringing." I wasn't joking. I don't have much of a sweet tooth, and I don't enjoy baking. There are so many other things to eat and make, like . . . risotto. So usually, when someone asks what they can bring to my house for a dinner party, my automatic reply is, "Dessert."

Every once in a while, though, the spirit moves me, and I decide to take on the challenge of making dessert all by myself. When I do, these are my tried and true company favorites: easy, delicious, and easy to make well in advance of company arriving.

PUMPKIN CHEESECAKE

V, NF	Serves 8–12	Prep Time: 20 minutes	Bake Time: 1 hour + 8 hours cooling

Okay, so I told you that one of the reasons I don't bake is because I don't have a sweet tooth. Which is true. But it's also true that I think this pumpkin cheesecake will be served in heaven and is the closest thing to ambrosia on this earth. I make this once a year, at Thanksgiving. I then proceed to eat a piece every single day until it's gone. Which is why I don't bake this particular dessert more than once a year.

2 cups gingersnap cookie crumbs
1/2 cup butter, melted
3 (8 ounce) blocks cream cheese, at room temperature
1 (15 ounce) can pumpkin puree
3 whole eggs plus 1 egg yolk
1/4 cup sour cream
1 1/2 cups sugar
1/2 teaspoon cinnamon
1/4 teaspoon ground nutmeg
1/8 teaspoon ground cloves
2 tablespoons flour
1 teaspoon vanilla extract

1. Preheat oven to 350° F.
2. Combine gingersnap crumbs and butter in a bowl. Mix well, until crumbs are moist. Pour into the bottom of a 9-inch springform pan and press until firm.
3. Using a stand mixer, beat cream cheese until smooth. Add sour cream, pumpkin, eggs, egg yolk, and sugar. Beat until combined.
4. Add spices and beat some more.
5. Lastly, add vanilla and flour. Beat until the mixture is uniformly smooth, stopping once or twice to scrape the bottom of the bowl if necessary.
6. Pour into the pan on top of gingersnap crust. Place in the oven on the center rack. Beneath it, place a 9 x 13-inch pan, half-filled with water. Bake for one hour.
7. When finished, turn oven off and leave the oven door open for 30–60 minutes. Remove from oven and let sit on the counter for 30 minutes more.
8. Cover tightly with plastic wrap and refrigerate overnight.

LEMON CAKE

V, NF	Serves: 8	Prep Time: 10 minutes	Bake Time: 20–25 minutes

In 2019, my dad got very sick. He'd been a little sick for a long time, but that was the first year we almost lost him—twice. Over the next five years, my dad cheated death again and again, until he finally passed in August of 2023. During those years, our little family drove the 630 miles between Pittsburgh, Pennsylvania, and Rock Island, Illinois, more times than I can count. Some years, we did the drive almost monthly.

All of which is my excuse for why my oldest son developed an obsession with Starbucks Lemon Bread before he was three years old. We ate on the road a lot during those years, and Starbucks was often the least bad of many bad options. After Dad died, though, and our road trips grew fewer, I began working on replicating the lemon bread at home, making a bread that would please Toby but without all the preservatives and chemicals. This lemon cake has done the trick.

1/2 cup sugar
4 tablespoons salted butter, softened
1/3 cup heavy whipping cream
2 eggs
3 lemons, zested and juiced
1 teaspoon vanilla extract
1 1/4 cups flour
2 teaspoons baking powder
1/4 teaspoon salt

Icing

1 cup powdered sugar
1 tablespoon milk
fresh raspberries (optional)

1. Preheat oven to 350° F. In a bowl, combine flour, baking powder, and salt. Set aside.
2. In a stand mixer, cream butter and sugar together. Add cream, eggs, vanilla, 2 tablespoons lemon zest, and 1/3 cup lemon juice. Beat until smooth.
3. To the batter, slowly add flour mixture, continuing to mix until combined.
4. Pour the batter into a 9-inch cake pan (either lined with parchment paper or greased with butter and dusted with flour). Bake for 20–25 minutes or until a fork comes out clean. Allow the cake to cool on a rack for 15 minutes.
5. While the cake cools, combine the powdered sugar and milk. Once the cake is cool, sprinkle with remaining lemon zest and a little more powdered sugar. Pour the icing over the top, dot with raspberries, and serve.

NO-BAKE CASHEW & SALTED CARAMEL ICE CREAM CAKE

V	Serves 10–12	Prep Time: 20 minutes active; 8–24 hours inactive

As a rule, I don't recommend stress eating. Stress baking, however, has its uses. Especially when part of that baking involves beating a bag full of gingersnaps to a pulp with a rolling pin. I mean, yes, you could reduce them to crumbs in a food processor, but then you might be tempted to eat your feelings later, when the ice cream cake is ready. Better to attack the crumbs first so you can properly enjoy the cake later.

Cake

- 30 gingersnap cookies
- 3 tablespoons butter
- 3/4 quart salted caramel ice cream, softened
- 3/4 cup heavy cream
- 1 heaping tablespoon powdered sugar
- 1 1/2 cups roasted salted cashews
- 1 cup caramel sauce

1. Beat heavy cream in a stand mixer (or with a hand-held one) until soft peaks form. Add powdered sugar and beat for another 30–60 seconds. Set aside.
2. To make the crust, place 30 or so gingersnaps in a food processor and pulse until small crumbs form. Alternately, place those same gingersnaps in a large, sealable, plastic bag. Place that bag in another plastic bag, then, pulverize with a rolling pin. (if it's been a rough week, I highly recommend this second method.)
3. Once you have finished crushing the cookies, reserve 1/4 cup of the cookie crumbs and set aside. Melt 3 tablespoons butter and combine with the remaining gingersnap crumbs. Press into a 9-inch round spring form pan.
4. Finally, using a rubber spatula, spread a full half-gallon of ice cream plus about another half of a half-gallon over the crust.
5. Roughly chop 3/4 cup cashews and scatter on top of the ice cream.
6. With a spatula, slather the whipped cream on top of the cashews.
7. Top the cake with the remaining 1/4 cup of cookie crumbs and cashews. Cover tightly with foil and freeze for at least 8 hours, preferably 24.
8. Before serving, top individual slices with caramel sauce.

VEGAN CHOCOLATE PUDDING

GF, DF, V, VG, NF	Serves 8	Prep Time: 3 minutes

Most of the time, if someone is coming over for dinner who can't have dairy or animal products, I serve fruit. Or non-dairy ice cream. There are lots of really excellent non-dairy ice creams out there, so this is an easy hosting call for me. Occasionally, though, if I have all the ingredients on hand, I make this vegan chocolate pudding. My former roommate Shannon introduced it to me years ago, and there are about five hundred variations of it floating around on the internet. This is my version.

4 very ripe, very soft bananas
2 very ripe (but still green) avocados
4 tablespoons cocoa powder
maple syrup (optional)

1. In a blender or processor, combine bananas, avocados, and cocoa powder and blend until smooth and creamy (adding a small amount of water 1 tablespoon at a time if necessary to move the blender along).
2. Taste, and if it is not sweet enough, add a small amount of syrup or an extra banana.
3. Chill until ready to serve.

SUSANNAH'S CHOCOLATE CHIP COOKIES

GF, V	Yield: 18–24 cookies	Prep Time: 5 minutes	Bake Time: 12 minutes

My husband insists these belong in the brunch chapter. Since they are higher in protein and lower in sugar than your average cookie, he believes they can be eaten for breakfast. I agree. They absolutely can. But they're still cookies and extremely popular when I take them into my children's preschool, so I am keeping them here, in the dessert chapter, where they rightfully belong.

- 1/2 cup butter, softened
- 1/2 cup raw sugar
- 2 eggs
- 1 teaspoon vanilla extract
- 1/2 teaspoon salt
- 1/2 teaspoon baking soda
- 3 cups almond flour or meal
- 2 cups or 1 (12 ounce) bag chocolate chips

1. Preheat oven to 375° F and line two baking sheets with parchment paper.
2. Cream butter, sugar, vanilla, and eggs.
3. Add dry ingredients; mix well.
4. Spoon dough or form into small balls and place on baking sheet.
5. Bake for 12 minutes or until they reach your desired level of doneness.

GINGERBREAD WITH LEMON SAUCE

NF	Serves 12	Prep Time: 15 minutes	Cook Time: 30–35 minutes

Because my teeth (like my soul) run to the salty, not sweet side, my favorite desserts have a touch of savory to them. This warm, spicy gingerbread cake, which came to me about twenty years ago, by way of one of my roommates, fits the bill perfectly.

Gingerbread

- 2 1/4 cups flour
- 1 1/2 teaspoons ground ginger
- 1 1/2 teaspoons cinnamon
- 1/2 teaspoon ground cloves
- 1/2 teaspoon ground nutmeg
- 1/2 teaspoon salt
- 2 tablespoons baking powder
- 2 large eggs
- 3/4 cup brown sugar
- 3/4 cup molasses
- 3/4 cup applesauce
- 1/2 teaspoon baking soda
- 1 cup boiling water

Lemon Sauce

- 1/2 cup butter
- 1 cup sugar
- 1/4 cup water
- 1 egg, beaten
- 3 tablespoons fresh lemon juice

1. Preheat oven to 350° F.
2. Sift together the first seven ingredients in a bowl and set aside.
3. In a separate bowl, beat eggs, sugar, molasses, and apple sauce. Slowly stir in flour mixture.
4. Dissolve baking soda in 1 cup of boiling water. Immediately stir into the cake batter.
5. Pour the batter into a greased 9 x 13-inch pan. Bake for 30–35 minutes or until the center is set and a toothpick inserted into the center comes out dry.
6. Allow the cake to cool for 15 minutes.
7. While the cake is cooling, make the lemon sauce. In a small saucepan, combine sugar, water, egg, and lemon juice. Cook over low heat, stirring constantly, until the mixture thickens. Add the butter, continuing to stir, until it melts completely into the lemon sauce.
8. Serve over warm slices of gingerbread.

SIMPLE BLACKBERRY & APPLE CRISP

GF, V	Serves 10	Prep Time: 10 Minutes	Bake Time: 40–45 minutes

This is my, "Oh no, someone asked me to bring the dessert!" standard. Fast. Easy. Transports well. The vanilla ice cream is optional . . . but not really.

6 cups fresh blackberries

2 large Granny Smith apples, cored and chopped

1/4 cup sugar

2 cups old-fashioned oats

1 cup almond flour or meal

1/2 cup packed brown sugar

1 cup roughly chopped pecans

3/4 cup or 12 tablespoons butter, melted (plus extra for greasing the baking dish)

vanilla ice cream

1. Preheat oven to 375° F.
2. Grease a 9×13 pan or 2.5 quart baking dish with butter.
3. Throw in your blackberries and chopped apples. Add granulated sugar and stir.
4. In a separate bowl, stir together the oats, almond flour, brown sugar and pecans. Spread on top of the fruit in the baking dish.
5. Pour the melted butter over the topping.
6. Bake for 40–45 minutes or until the oat crumble is golden.
7. Serve warm or room temperature, topped with ice cream.

CHOCOLATE CASHEW CLUSTERS

GF, V	Yield: 70 large clusters	Cook Time: 5–10 minutes	Spooning Out Time: A long while

When I was a little girl, I lived for my grandma's chocolate peanut clusters. Then, in my early twenties, I went and developed a peanut allergy. Now I live only if I don't eat my grandma's peanut clusters. One bite and no more breathing for me. Fortunately, cashews and I get along just fine—so fine that even if peanuts didn't make my throat close up, I'd still prefer this adaptation of my childhood favorite.

- 2 pounds white candy or baking bark
- 3 cups (18 ounces) semisweet chocolate chips
- 4 ounces dark baking chocolate
- 9 cups (3 pounds) cashews
- a full roll of wax paper

1. Spread out wax paper on your countertop . . . and table . . . and any other flat surface you can find. This recipe makes a ton of candy.
2. Once you've papered your kitchen with wax paper, take a large, heavy-bottomed pot and melt all the chocolate (white, dark, semi-sweet) over low (low!) heat, stirring continuously.
3. When the candy is completely melted, remove from heat, add cashews, and combine well.
4. Drop by the spoonful onto wax paper and allow to cool and harden.
5. Store in an airtight container in the refrigerator for up to a month.

NO-BAKE PROTEIN COOKIES

GF, DF, V	Makes 48 Cookies	Prep Time: 15 Minutes

When I was a little girl, few things excited me more than arriving home from school to discover that my mom had made no-bake cookies. They were the tastiest. But not the healthiest. So for the past few years, I have been playing around with various protein cookie recipes, attempting to make one that tastes just as good but is healthier. This is the fruit of those efforts. Chris loves them so much, he insists on getting his own separate batch, which he then hides from the kids (and won't even share with me!)

- 2 cups almond butter
- 1/2 cup honey
- 1/2 cup coconut oil
- 4 cups instant or quick-cooking oats (gluten-free if needed)
- 1/2 cup coffee- or chocolate-flavored protein powder
- 2 cups roughly chopped cashews
- 1/2 cup shredded coconut
- 1 cup chocolate chips

1. Melt the coconut oil.
2. Mix all the ingredients together.
3. Drop by the spoonful onto a sheet pan lined with wax paper or parchment paper.
4. Freeze for 30 minutes. Transfer cookies to a large container and store in the refrigerator for a week or the freezer for up to a month.

"MAMA"

My son Toby's first word—the first word he repeated over and over again, with meaning and purpose and even on command—was "Mama." He whispered it as he woke up in the morning and as he fell asleep at night. He shouted it when I walked into a room or when he pinched his fingers in the cabinet door. He even sang it to himself as he played in one corner while I worked in another. Everywhere he went, it was "Mama, Mama, Mama."

Then one day, my husband and I realized something. When Toby was saying "Mama," he wasn't always talking about me. He wasn't just calling or singing or dreaming of the woman who held him and fed him and rocked him to sleep. Sometimes, he was calling or singing or dreaming about something else, for "Mama" was also his word for "food."

Toby said "Mama" when what he meant was, "I am hungry. Give me something to eat." He also said "Mama" when he was pleased with what he'd been given, when he wanted to say, "I am happy. I am satisfied. This is good."

"Mama" was both Toby's "please" and Toby's "thank you," his "I am empty" and his "I am full." He knew whenever he said "Mama," what he needed would come, whether that need was for comfort, healing, affection, strength, milk, or just a quick smile to reassure him all was well.

Which, of course, is just as it should be. Only, I didn't know if it would be that way for me.

Toby, like all our babies, was adopted. But he was the first—the one who made me "Mama." And I didn't know, both before we brought him home and for some time afterward, what the bond between us would look like. I knew I would love him before I met him. I knew I would die for him the moment I heard his first cries. But I didn't know if he would feel the same way about me. Would he see me as his own? Would I be to him what other mothers are to the babies born from their bodies and not just their hearts?

I spent so many hours, days, and weeks asking myself those questions, worrying the answer would be no. Even after he came home with us, I worried. Chris said I had no reason for that. Toby held fast to me from the first. I was the one he wanted. I was the one to whom he clung.

He knew whenever he said "Mama," what he needed would come, whether that need was for comfort, healing, affection, strength, milk, or just a quick smile to reassure him all was well.

I was the one whose face he always sought out, wanting to press it against his own. During much of Toby's first year of life, we spent hours like that, walking cheek to cheek about the house. Even today, that's how he likes to cuddle with me, his cheek pressed firmly against my own, while his now gangly legs dangle close to the floor.

During those early months, however, I worried just the same. It wasn't my blood that fed him in utero. It wasn't my milk that helped him grow and thrive after birth. It was my arms that held him and my voice that calmed him, but I was so very worried that wouldn't be enough. I was so very worried I wouldn't be enough.

Then he gave food my name. And I stopped worrying.

That was almost six years ago now, and Toby's use of language has advanced well beyond calling food and everything to do with it "Mama." But I still treasure that memory, both for what it showed me about our bond and for what it underlined for me about motherhood.

Whether a woman has ten children or none at all, there is something about food and the feminine that is inextricably linked. Not simply because women generally (but certainly not always) do more cooking than men in the home, but more because women can do something men can't. We can become food. It's a woman's blood that nourishes the child in her womb. It's her milk that nourishes her child at her breast. Our life is poured into them. Our strength is given to them. And in that, we image Christ like no man can.

That likeness is a tremendous gift. Even if some of us never get the chance to do it, even if no babies' hearts ever rest under our own, the latent ability is still there. In potential, if not in fact, we are like Jesus. We too are made to be a type of Eucharist.

I think about this likeness the most when I am in my kitchen, where I typically cook three meals a day for my children. I enjoy cooking, but even I struggle at times with how much time, energy, and patience it takes to feed these growing babes, whose tastes are less predictable than a teenager's moods. I also struggle with the mess this cooking makes. I look forward to the day when I can hand off the post-dinner cleanup to Toby, Becket, and Ellie. But we're not there yet, and the constant cycle of cooking and cleaning remains exhausting.

> *Whether a woman has ten children or none at all, there is something about food and the feminine that is inextricably linked.*

I keep cooking though. Partly because someone must; the children must be fed, and the kitchen is not my husband's comfort zone. But also because in this constant act of cooking and serving, washing and wiping, I get to be like my Lord.

Every day, in every Mass, the sacrifice Christ made on Calvary is made present to us. He is there, on the altar, offering to us the same Body that hung on the Cross once for all, feeding us with his Body, Blood, Soul, and Divinity, re-forming our hearts into the image of his.

And every day, I stand in my kitchen, pouring myself out in a different way. Cooking is my perpetual sacrifice. My body is not food for my children. It never has been. But every morning, noon, and night, I still get to use my body to feed them. My mind, my heart, my strength, my energy, my creativity, and my tenacity—all of that, all of me, goes into every dish I make. And when my children take and eat that food, I believe some of what I poured into the meal passes through it to them. That is to say, I believe that when they eat what I've made, my mind, my heart, my strength, my energy, my creativity, and my tenacity, in some mysterious way, become theirs, too. It becomes a part of who they are and a part of who they will become.

In the kitchen, I have found intimacy with Christ, who gives his life to us in the form of food. I've also found intimacy with generations of women who came before me, a great feminine company who have nourished souls as they nourished bodies, pouring themselves out so the ones they loved could grow and thrive. It is a privilege to be among their number. It is, in some ways, one of the deepest blessings of my life. Years ago, cooking for friends and roommates gave me a way to live my vocation to motherhood long before I became a mother. Now, it gives me a way to live the feminine call to nourish life, even though my own body was never capable of bearing life.

There are many ways to live motherhood. Plenty of good mothers exist who are no happier in the kitchen than my husband is. Nevertheless, what a sacred space for women the kitchen can be. It is holy ground, where love can become food and motherhood can become nourishment and every woman, even those of us whose wombs are barren, can become mothers. Toby knew what he was about when he settled on one word, "Mama," to express hunger and satisfaction, love and nourishment, strength and healing, joy and thanksgiving. Only one other world in all the word can do the same. And "Eucharist" would have been a bit much for a six-month-old.

ACKNOWLEDGMENTS

No cookbook is ever an author's own. No recipe is ever an author's own either. Like music, every recipe is a variation on a theme, with cooks borrowing bits from others, then adapting and improvising as they make it their own. The recipes in this cookbook are no exception. It's filled with favorites, adapted to varying degrees, from my father, Gary Stimpson; my grandmother, Mary Ann Miller; my aunt, Amy Daube; my mother's dear friend, Linda Moore; and my friends (in real life and online), Christina Corzine, Britt Fisk, Elizabeth Scalia, Janet Easter, and Susannah Pearce.

I'm also grateful to Caitlin Renn for her beautiful photos of my family, as well as her work on the book cover and section covers; Melissa Girard's patient and painstaking editing; and Emily Morelli's beautiful design. I'm also grateful to Joachim Gawryolek for his technical help with the recipe photos. Additional thanks is due to Edyta McNichol and Katie Takats for their editorial assistance, and especially to Caroline Rock and Jenna St. Hilaire for their excellent proofreading on this beast of a cookbook. I'm afraid they got more work than they bargained for!

This cookbook would never be in your hands if not for the enthusiastic support of my readers on Instagram, who supported our adoptions of Becket and Ellie in 2020 and 2021, and received an early digital version of *Around the Catholic Table* as my thanks. Without their love of the recipes and requests for a hardback version that they could give to family and friends, this cookbook would still live only in cyberspace (and be much smaller, with fewer recipes and fewer essays than it now has).

Last but not least, I'm grateful to my husband and children—for testing the recipes and putting up with late dinners and a very messy kitchen as I photographed every single thing we ate for months—and for all the early testers of these recipes in my Pittsburgh and Steubenville kitchens: the Stapletons, Corzines, Schwartzes, Crowes, Longs, Carpenters, Mathews, Mitchells, McKeegans, Leonards, Chodorowskis, Bonjours, Garlands, Wears, Turks, McManamons, Shrakes, and Weeks, plus Shannon Walsh, Victoria Sanborn, Lisa Ferguson, Theresa Wichert, Haydn Ward and every other guest at my Thursday Night Dinners of old. I love you and miss you all and look forward to feasting with you again, whether in this life or the next.